Reviews

NAMI Utah (National Alliance for the Mentally Ill)

Long before you have reached the final period on the final page, Andy Hogan has become your son or your brother. His eloquent writing skills and his sense of humor make this book very readable. Masterfully Andy makes you part of his early adulthood where excellence is the standard and obstacles are there to be conquered. As his goals become more and more ambitious and only perfection in all things at all times seems acceptable, you wonder expectantly where life will take this remarkable young man. It comes as no surprise that he is entrusted with an enormous challenge. Ignorant of his dangerous "inheritance," he pushes more and more towards accomplishment until mental illness shatters his promising life. The reader will hardly forget the anguish and horrors Andy's book describes both from his recollections and from those who were present during the episodes. Even after recovery, Andy's life will remain overshadowed by his illness, but as his impressive book proves, a meaningful life can be found because mental illnesses are medically treatable.

Richard Davidson MD, Board Certified Psychiatrist

Stigma in our society viciously labels sufferers of mental illness as "hopelessly ill people who walk the streets alone talking to themselves that are beyond hope and help." Andy Hogan's book dispels these myths. Andy wasn't a lonely, "crazy," homeless person. On the contrary. In high school, he was popular, athletic, and loved by a beautiful girl. On his volunteer mission he was highly successful and well respected. No one ever suspected a mental breakdown of such intense magnitude could strike someone like him. It did. It does.

In my profession I have seen many highly regarded youth who secretly suffer deep depression or who, unexpectedly to all, fall prey to delusions or extreme mania. Such would do well to read Andy's story. The lesson they will learn dissolves the myth that mental illness is untreatable and hopeless. When Andy finally faces his bipolar disorder humbly and honestly, he allows himself the help of professionals, proper and consistent medication, and the unyielding love of his parents. There he finds hope, relief, and stability.

BIPOLAR DISORDER IN TRUTH

Understanding the Refiner's Fire

Andrew S. Hogan

ISBN 10: 0-9708572-3-3
ISBN 13: 978-09708572-3-1

BEAR CANYON PRESS, LLC
Centerville, Utah

CONTENTS

Foreword

The Chinese have a saying: "Zhen Jin Bu Pa Huo Lian." The translation is: "true gold does not fear the refiner's fire." The saying has inspired me with its wisdom and power ever since I returned home after serving a mission in Taichung, Taiwan. I shared that saying with my Special Teams Coach of the Philadelphia Eagles, John Harbaugh, and he liked it enough to have T-shirts and shorts made up with the Chinese writing of the saying on them for the entire team. It was a perfect fit. My teammates loved the beauty and intrigue of Chinese writing as well as the inspirational message behind the words.

It is one thing to talk tough and sound fearless by reciting a classic Chinese proverb in the face of adversity. It is quite another thing to be tough and fearless in the face of adversity. If you are like me, you probably need someone to show you the way. I was lucky enough to serve in the same mission at the same time with Andy Hogan. He was one of the noble missionaries who had enough courage himself to share his fire of faith with me in a way that inspired me to face some of the early challenges of being a Taiwan missionary.

During our language training in Provo, Utah Andy and I lived together for one month before we headed over to Taiwan. It was during that month together while getting to know Andy that I started to appreciate his gift to speak the language and his love for the other missionaries. He inspired those around him to stare into the face of adversity and march forward.

What adversity can there be as a Taiwan missionary? Learning the language, adjusting to the culture, memorizing the 60 or so pages of missionary lessons in Mandarin, and trying to love others with the same love that Jesus Christ loves us with, just to name a few. During my first few days in the training center Andy and his companion, Ken Bown, were so encouraging to me that I felt as if it was possible for me to learn to speak the difficult language as well as translators for the U.N. I could also feel a Christ-like love and concern from Andy that made me feel comfortable, as if he was a big brother who had my back.

When I arrived in Taiwan and was assigned to the city of Yuan Lin, I attacked the requirement to memorize the missionary lessons with all the fire and energy I had. It only took a short while to realize that I had just run into a major brick wall, one that hit harder than linebackers in the NFL. Memorizing the lessons in Mandarin was a true test. I felt so discouraged. I talked to Andy and just like in the training center, he was inspirational. He told me that he would pray for me. Once again, he had my back.

It was a month later when I saw Andy at a church gathering and he asked me how I was doing. He told me that he had been praying for me, and because of his sincerity, I could not hide my emotions. I cried tears of gratitude and appreciation. His prayers had helped me conquer the brick wall of memorizing the lessons. I felt so honored to have his help in the midst of my trial.

A few months later, when I found out that Andy had a chemical imbalance while he was working in the city, Chao Chou, and consequently was sent back to America, it broke my heart. I knew how much he loved being in Taiwan. My companion at the time was his former companion: Ken Bown. We prayed for Andy as he prayed for me. We made a tape for him where we sang songs and tried our best to let him know how much we cared about him. His absence left a huge void in our mission.

Now, two decades later, I am so glad that Andy has the courage to open himself up to the world by telling his personal story. I love the way he writes and describes life with nature, music and his own creativity. I have read this entire book, and believe it would be a great read for anyone who desires to understand what really goes on in the mind of someone suffering with chronic bipolar disorder, and how he learned to live a fairly normal life despite it.

By reading this story of Andy Hogan's life, I have learned more about how much our Savior loves us. God didn't abandon Andy during Andy's extreme manic breakdowns or deep depressive episodes. The Lord was simply refining His gold. I feel fortunate that I was able to serve with Andy Hogan in Taiwan. Our mission president, Kent Watson, taught us to surround ourselves with greatness. Standing next to Andy Hogan, I was.

Since music is a huge part of Andy's life, I will finish with one of my favorite hymns. It gives me so much strength and courage to face the refining process that we all go through.

Lead, kindly Light,
amid the encircling gloom; Lead thou me on!
The night is dark, and I am far from home; Lead thou me on!
Keep thou my feet; I do not ask to see
The distant scene—one step enough for me.

盧高偉

Chad Lewis,
Philadelphia Eagles, Tight End (Retired)
Taichung, Taiwan missionary

Preface

    This book is based on a true story. The names have been changed except for those who gave permission. I would like to offer special thanks to those who dug in their journals and memory banks to help recreate the incidents. While writing these memories and corresponding with these individuals, I was reminded how God surrounded me with competent and caring people at a time when my life was as fragile as my health. I will always be grateful for their life-saving efforts and life-changing examples.

    I would also like to thank my neighbor and friend, Gary Flood, for his many hours and invaluable help in proofreading and editing. Also, feichang ganxie ni (heartfelt thanks) to my mission hero, Chad Lewis, for his powerful foreword. If you think he's good with shoulder pads and a pigskin, you should see him battle for souls while wearing a tie and carrying a set of scriptures.

    Finally, I would like to dedicate this book to the millions of people who suffer from bipolar disorder or any other mental illness as well as those who love them. This is a story of hope. It's a story of someone who believes the war can be won no matter how brutal it becomes. Never quit fighting. Never lose hope. Life is worth living.

Andy Hogan

— Andy Hogan —

Chapter 1
The Birth of my Bipolar Disorder

When other Americans hear that I served a religious mission in Taiwan, they often ask me to recite something in Chinese. "Jia jia you ben nan nian de jing," I say.

"What does it mean?" they ask.

"It's one of my favorite Chinese idioms," I answer. "Directly translated it means, 'every home has a story of difficulty.' The English equivalent could be, 'everyone carries unseen crosses.'"

"Oh, that's so true," they reply. Then they all look at me, laugh, and say, "Well, it's true of everyone except Andy."

Most people who know me think I'm an exception to the saying. They think I'm the one who always has everything going his way. I'm that guy with the easy life who never suffers or struggles.

Once when I was introduced to a friend of my parents, she made the comment, "I've heard about you. You are the perfect all-American boy. As a youth you were popular in school. You were a basketball and running star. Now, you have a good, cushy job in your family business. You are an active leader in your community and church. You probably married your high school sweetheart and are living happily ever after raising your cute, healthy children."

On the outside, everything looks fine and dandy. Okay, some things about me are a little peculiar. Some think it's strange to see me driving down the street, alone, talking into a tape recorder. But when they ask my friends about it, they always smile and reply, "He sends tapes to his best friend Yoner in Taiwan. Everyone who knows him has heard him talk about his buddy from the Orient he met on his mission."

After I was married and we moved into our first home, our neighbors thought it odd to see lights on inside my house every night at midnight or even later. But now, they're all used to it. In between yawns, they say, "Andy is down on the computer again, pounding out another poem."

The next day, at an hour closer to lunchtime than breakfast, when I finally roll out of the house to go to work, my neighbors think it's normal to see me with an unshaven face and a ball cap on to hide my unwashed hair. As I drive by, they smile and wave as if everything is peaches, cream, and jellybeans.

My coworkers have also grown accustomed to my seemingly peculiar points. Once, at a company party, while observing me from the dance floor, one of the spouses asked her husband, "What's the matter with him? He hardly said anything during dinner and now he just sits there looking too tired to dance with the rest of us."

My coworker answered, "Nothing's wrong with him. He's always that way. It's just how he is."

So, for the most part, everyone thinks I'm a normal guy with a normal life. Everything looks cool and controlled...until–and it always seems to happen at the most inopportune times like neighborhood socials or extended in-law family reunions–they hear me make a comment about my mission in Montana. "I thought you served your mission in Taiwan," they observe inquisitively.

Right about then, all surrounding conversations stop and everyone turns to listen. My reply is always the same, "Oh, I got sick, came home from Taiwan, and finished in Montana."

Sometimes the conversation stops there; other times they ask that all-probing question, "What did you get?"

I make a joke of it: "Oh, I got the great gomboo." Or I'll say, "It's a bizarre Oriental disease called shen jing bing," knowing they don't understand Chinese. If it's Chinese people who don't speak English well, I say it in pig-Latin: "Iay entway azycray."

Even with uncomfortable humor, curiosity is usually stronger than courtesy laughs, and they ask for an explanation in their native tongue. At this point I usually tell them, "Well, I found out that I have a chemical imbalance when I had a nervous breakdown. I came home from Taiwan and was then reassigned to finish in Montana." Usually that information is plenty, and they don't ask to know any more-ever again.

Sometimes though, when I'm with close friends or other caring company and the "I thought you served your mission in Taiwan" question arises, I respond more openly. I tell them I have bipolar disorder or manic depressive disorder.

I never knew I had it until that dark day on my mission in Taiwan. With down-to-earth friends and family it isn't uncomfortable to use casual language. To say I went crazy, I lost touch, I freaked, or as one of my mission companions put it, "Dude, you were totally whacked."

Whatever you call it, when it happened, several of my fellow missionaries and the mission president dragged me to a hospital where I was given injections that made me sleep for what felt like weeks. When I finally woke up, sane again, I found myself back in Utah where I then spent an anxious month in the psychiatric ward of a hospital in Provo.

I was subsequently reassigned to the Billings Montana Mission where I suffered another breakdown. Following more shots and an eternal night locked in the psychiatric holding room of a hospital in Bozeman, I limped home again for a few weeks. Then, determined not to quit, I bounced back to Montana to try one more time. After a very close call to another breakdown, I decided it was time to come home for good-six months short of the two years I had planned to serve my mission.

That's the short version of the story. It's easy to tell. The long version is, at least for me, deeply complex, confusing, and even scary. It involves the deepest thoughts, the darkest repression, as well as the highest bliss I have known. It includes a story of a supreme sacrifice rewarded with true love. It is also a story of how a beautiful friendship was built between two people from opposite sides of the world. I haven't dared to face the long version of this story for over ten years now. But I feel the time has come to tell it.

I'm finally ready to go back, look my history right in the eyes, with sane eyes this time, and come to understanding and peace with it. I believe that by reading my "story of difficulty," others dealing with bipolar disorder can avoid my ordeal. Maybe the burden of your unseen cross can be lightened as you see how I have learned to bear mine. Of course, parents, family, friends, teachers and leaders also need to learn about mental illness. That way, should the need arise, they will have an idea of what is happening (and what is not happening) and how to help.

My story is for all these. It's a story that says, "There is hope! I suffered in as great of extreme as any story you have heard of. Yet, I still believe in and love God. I am living a normal and productive life. I am not cured, but I am making it. You can too!"

When I stumbled onto that homebound plane, I'm sure my mission president and the young missionaries I left behind in Montana, who carried me to the hospital while I thrashed and screamed at the sky just days before, never would have guessed my life could be where it is now.

Since then, I have married and stayed married for twelve years and counting. We have two healthy and happy children. I hold a full-time job that allows my wife to stay home-our own home, not our parents'-with the children. I am a Boy Scout Master. I coached little league basketball. I ran a marathon. I'm not bragging. I'm making an announcement that it is possible for people with severe, chronic mental illness to live meaningful, fulfilling, and even productive lives! Some of us even crack jokes once in a while.

What I'm saying is this story has a happy ending! When I look back now, I can laugh about what happened. Yeah, I really did bite another missionary on the leg. His scar is still there! Yep, I thought the toilet at an airport was a baptismal font. I played in the water. It's funny now. I'm not offended if you laugh. Let's laugh together. We all need precious laughter.

Sure, it was serious then-very serious. One of the doctors in Bozeman Montana told my mission president that people suffering breakdowns as severe as mine take years to recover. He said, "Andy may never be the same again."

I wish I could know where that doctor is today. I would like to look him in the eyes, with sane eyes this time, and say, "You were wrong about me. Ok, so I spit swear words at you while I slithered on the hospital floor like a snake. You said I was a disgrace to my church and myself. I say statements like that make you a disgrace to professional health care givers. Look at me now. I'm sane. I didn't commit suicide. I graduated from college. I'm supporting a family and living a fairly normal life. It's true I'm not the same person as before the breakdown. I'm an improved person. In the flames of the roaring fire, I have been refined and bettered."

Mental illness is not something spoken of openly. It's a subject too many people fear. It's like a badminton racket with a broken string. You know the one. It's stuffed away in the back of your dark, dusty closet. Everyone knows it's there, but no one likes to talk about it for fear they will have to use it. So, when it's time to play, one person is always forced out of the game because no one wants the racket with the "loose string." Why not take the racket out, examine it, and tie a knot in the string? It may not be perfect, but at least everyone will get to play!

My racket string hasn't always been broken. From a very young age, however, I had a small idea of the great pain involved when it snaps. At first, it wasn't my own string that exploded; it was my mother's. I was still in elementary school when she suffered her first extreme manic episode. Back then we called it a nervous breakdown.

Late one night, yelling in my parents' room awoke me from my peaceful slumber. I sneaked to their bedroom doorway and spied as my dad tried desperately to figure out what was wrong with Mother. She had panic in her eyes and was shouting nonsense words about angels, trumpets, and Satan. When Grandpa came to help she yelled out, "There he is! There he is! Cast him away!" My dad didn't know she was suffering an extreme manic episode; he thought she was possessed with an evil spirit. In terror I listened as he said over and over: "...in Jesus' name I command this evil spirit to leave the room."

It took a long time for my dad to realize she was ill and not possessed. Finally, he did the right thing and took her to the hospital. I suppose it would be easy to confuse someone suffering with extreme mania to be possessed with an evil spirit. Repression is unrestrained and extreme emotions burst out viciously. You can't reason with the person. It's as if something else is controlling him or her. Still, according to my experience, just like you can't start a car by shoving an apple slice in the ignition, you can't stop a manic episode by casting out devils. Keys are for ignitions, smashed apples make yummy sauce, and prescribed medication works for manic psychosis.

Just as important as the proper medication, a companion treatment for bipolar disorder is professional counseling. Mother eventually found a compatible counselor who helped her through the toughest times. Sadly, no one ever counseled us children about what happened to Mother or how we should deal with it. We were just told she was sick and we needed to be quiet around her. She came home after a few weeks in the hospital. Though the manic episode had passed, she was far from cured.

Every day I watched in disgust as Mother slumped on the couch, reading her scriptures or humming hymns, all the while crying and crying, hour after hour. When Dad came home from work, she would talk to him about her failures as a wife and mother, how evil was out to get her family, and how hopeless and helpless she felt. Some nights, when the depression switched to mania, she would take Dad into their room and talk for hours about her interpretations of scriptures and writings of church leaders. Sometimes she would get so worked up by what she was saying, she would start yelling like a roadside preacher. Even though their door was closed, we children were unable to sleep until she quieted down.

As children we were left to guess for ourselves what was wrong with Mother and how she could get better. My cruel adolescent theory was that she was too "goodie goodie." It was all in her head. If she would just chill out, get up and exercise, or just get up and do something, rather than lie on the couch reading scriptures and singing hymns all day, she would feel better. I didn't realize when I told her that, it was the equivalent of telling someone with a broken leg just getting up and walking would solve the problem.

Her problem was not "all in her head." Just like a broken bone, it was a physical deficiency in her body that needed treatment. A teacher wouldn't say to a student who was suffering from a diabetic attack, "Snap out of it and get to work! You just need an attitude adjustment." No, the teacher would kindly and quickly get proper food or medication for the student.

My mother's depression was no different than the diabetic student. The thing she needed most from her family was love and understanding, not criticism and disgust. I think it would have helped my attitude if, as a family, we could have talked about our feelings and the situation openly. But how do you talk about something nobody understands?

They say the best way to understand a person is to walk a mile in his or her shoes. I never dared to think I would learn firsthand exactly how powerful her illness was. I grew up a normal child, with happy times and sad times. I had times of hyperactivity and times of dragging emotions. These are the symptoms of the disorder, but they are also characteristics of all children. Discerning the difference between a normal child and someone who has this illness is what makes bipolar disorder so tricky to diagnose.

Bipolar disorder is believed to be hereditary. However, none of my three brothers and sister have ever been diagnosed with it. Somehow, I was the only one who got the glowing gene. Early on, we all seemed like healthy, "normal" children. Neither schoolteachers nor Boy Scout leaders ever suspected I was any different than the other Hogan kids. No one ever dreamed I would one day relive my mother's worst nightmare.

Chapter 2
Grandiose Love

The word "bipolar" denotes two extremes, like the South Pole and Santa's place. The two poles I bounce up and down from, like that jolly old elf going up and down chimneys, trying not to get burned in the process, are mania and depression. Since we're talking about jolly and cheer, let's talk about mania first.

When manic my mind feels sharp, alert and explosively creative. Thoughts and ideas seem to be of utmost importance and carry eternal significance. Mania makes me feel motivated, passionate, enthusiastic and "pumped," as I used to say as a youth.

Mania usually happens at night when I should be sleeping. However, in the manic phase, sleep is the last thing on my mind. My brain is too occupied with superhuman ideas and plans. These "grandiose" plans didn't drop on me all at once. Starting at childhood, they grew in my mind as I grew in stature.

The earliest "super" plan I remember was when I was around eight or nine years old. I wanted to invent a Spiderman web shooter that could clip onto my wrist and be able to shoot out a web so I could swing from trees and buildings just like Spiderman. Many intricate details for my invention came during sleepless nights from hours of focused thought.

There were several such plans and, of course, none of them ever happened. Because I was a child no one suspected my plans were grandiose or even abnormal. Children love to use their imagination and it's very normal for them to do so. Wasn't the best part of the TV show Mr. Rogers' Neighborhood when the trolley took viewers to "The Land of Make-believe"? All kids have imagination. It's a wonderful thing. My trolley, rolling between reality and make-believe, had a track that weakened with each year. As I grew into adolescent years my grandiose plans mutated from childhood fantasies into impossible self-expectations.

For example, during my high school years I heard a plethora of pep talks from coaches and successful athletes who said, "You can do anything." "The sky is the limit." "The only limitations you have are the limitations you put on yourself." "You can reach any height if you set a goal and climb hard enough."

The pep talks and clichés excited my mind and convinced me that I could do anything. With this in mind, my senior year I came up with a plan to be the fastest high school miler in Utah's history. Not only would I win state, but I would also be the first high school student in Utah to break the four-minute mile.

This was my line of thinking and I seriously believed I could do it if I had a goal and worked hard enough. Forget that, up until then, I hadn't broken a five-minute mile. My plan was quite simple: improve two seconds each time I raced. Just two seconds per race-how easy, and it mapped out perfectly that by the time of the state meet I would run a 3.58 mile, win state, break (more like shatter) the state record, and who knows, maybe even qualify for the Olympics, sponsors, and all the babes I could handle. As they said, "the sky is the limit." Why didn't I think of this plan before?

You can guess what happened. I worked my tail-end off...for about six months. My first race time was around five minutes and ten seconds-right where I had planned. The next race I improved exactly two seconds. "It's going to work!" I screamed in my mind. "Bring on the reporters."

The next race I improved more than two seconds and I actually broke the five-minute mile for the first time. The fourth race had about the same time as the third. "That's okay," I thought, "no big deal. I'll just take four seconds off the next race." The fifth race came. Same time, same reaction. "That's okay, I'll just take six seconds off the next race." And on and on it went. I never felt satisfied with small improvements because of the huge hole I felt I was in. My fastest time was four minutes and 43 seconds, ten seconds short of even qualifying for the state meet.

At the end of the year my parents and coaches all complimented me on a great season. Teammates signed my yearbook saying they looked up to me because I had run extra laps when everyone else had quit. It's sad that inwardly I wouldn't accept praise. I felt I was a failure and missed my goal because I didn't work hard enough.

Now, I look back at my stubborn, perfectionist mindset and laugh. I was so blind to an incredible accomplishment. In less than a year, I improved around 30 seconds in my mile time! What if an Olympic mile runner improved that much in a year?

Beside grandiose plans, another characteristic of mania is over-concentrated or obsessive thinking. This means when I got something on my mind, I couldn't get it out. Whether it was a song, a past argument, a movie, or just a hyper-hamster-in-the-whizzing-wheel thought, such round and round thinking caused much loss of sleep.

Obsessive thinking began when I was still quite young. I remember lying on my bed looking out the window at the stars, wondering about the end of the universe. This led to thoughts of eternal life. I had been taught that after I died, eventually my body and spirit would come back together, and this was called resurrection. After the resurrection, I would live forever. As I failed to comprehend how long forever was, I felt overwhelmed. The surrounding darkness and weight of an endless universe seemed to press down on my heart and stomach. I felt like I was going crazy. In tears I trudged across the hall into my parent's room, woke them up and burst out with something like, "We're never going to die!"

After I explained myself to my startled parents, I remember my dad lovingly responding, "What is a boy your age doing thinking about a deep subject like this in the middle of the night? Come lie down with us." My mother rubbed my back as we talked about it. They told me there are some things in this life that we just don't understand. Their words weren't comforting, but their warm bed, gentle touch, and soft voices were, and soon I fell asleep.

Sleep. Okay, now let's slow our thinking way down, talk slowly, and discuss the other extreme of the bipolar scale: depression. The earliest I can remember symptoms of depression was when I was ten or 11 years old. While walking toward the laundry room, I forgot what I was going to get because of an intense feeling or weight deep in my gut. I interpreted it to be worry. I stopped and stood there for a long time, trying to remember what I was worried about. It never came to me.

Over time my mind started subconsciously matching mental reasons with the physical "down" feelings. Usually the reasons it came up with were worry or unnecessary guilt. I say "unnecessary" because guilt can be healthy or unhealthy. I had both types, and really didn't know the difference. The healthy guilt motivated me to repent or inspired me to become a better person. The unhealthy guilt hurt my self-esteem and dragged me down into depression.

For example: In school one day I walked by a trashcan. There was a wad of paper lying on the floor next to it, where, like many of my basketball shots, someone had missed. "I should pick that up," I thought to myself. As I walked away, a cloud of guilt swarmed around my mind like the smell of the rotten eggs we used to throw at the side of the barn. I suddenly felt disqualified for heaven because I didn't pick it up. When the stench of guilt and thoughts of my "sin" became too unbearable, I finally turned around, stomped over, picked it up, and slam-dunked it into the trash bin.

Then there was the worrying. I worried my parents or siblings were going to die. I worried my dad would lose his job (even though his dad owned the company). I worried about my body suddenly growing a deformity. I worried about what I would be when I grew up. My brain constantly searched for things to worry about and, if it couldn't find a reason, I found myself worrying about not worrying. Fun, huh?

As a teenager I never associated my worry and guilt with a disorder; I just knew they were always there. They were heavy baggage I became so accustomed to lugging around all the time, I didn't feel normal without them. In reality the heavy baggage was depression. My mind incorrectly assigned guilt and worry from imperfect living in order to justify the constant "heavy" feeling.

I never received comments from others noticing symptoms of mania or depression until high school. One cool, autumn evening I met a radiant redhead at a home football game. We had a blast cheering for our team, jumping up and down on the bleachers, and laughing loudly so we couldn't hear the upset comments of irritated parents behind us who preferred to watch the game while sitting.

The next time I saw her was a couple of days later when we passed each other in the hall at school. She quietly walked up to me and asked, "What's wrong?" Her words confused me. I didn't feel anything was wrong. Why did she say that? The next time I saw her, she got a deep, concerned look on her face and said, "You were so happy at the football game and now you're so sad! What's wrong?" If I could go back and answer her question now, I would tell her that I had been on a manic high the night of the football game and now I was in my normal, mild depression mode. That's why I looked sad. But I didn't know, I just thought she was weird and she probably thought I was mental. If that's what she thought, she was right, but I wouldn't know it for a few more years.

From that time on, I began to notice people constantly commenting that I looked tired or sad—even when I wasn't tired or said. They sometimes asked me if I was okay. Over time I learned just to snap back, "Oh, I'm just tired." With this annoyed, standard answer no one ever pressed the issue further, and I always managed to end the conversation without digging where it hurt or allowing others to see (or help with) my true, misunderstood feelings. Come to find out, irritability is also a symptom of bipolar disorder.

Speaking of avoiding pain, another symptom of bipolar disorder, which started pecking at me in my late youth, was what I termed: "scary thoughts." I later learned the medical term to be "intrusive thoughts." I think my term is a more accurate description. Many psychiatrists and social workers believe that scary thoughts are actually mental distractions. They say the brain is like a child who is attacked and hurt by the barnyard rooster. The child will never go to the barnyard again without throwing a fit. Depression is the barnyard rooster. Rather than deal with its accompanying pain and anguish over and over, the brain learns to "throw fits" in order to occupy itself with more powerful and controlling thoughts.

My mother thinks differently. She believes scary thoughts are put in my head by the devil. I don't know which is the case or if it's a combination of both. I do know that demonic thoughts started haunting me during my late teenage years.

So what were they? I guess the best way to describe them would be to say that somehow my brain got stuck on the question, "What is the worst possible thing I could do or say in any given situation?" Answers to this horrifying question randomly whizzed through my head like the time my buddy, who was always trying to be funny, foolishly snuck a handful of .22 bullets into our campfire. We all jumped for cover behind rocks and trees when the bullets heated up and started shooting through the air. Zing; a suicidal thought whispered, "Jump!" when I stood on top of a 500-foot cliff overlooking Lake Powell. Zang; a violent thought growled, "Punch him where it hurts!" when my math teacher walked past my desk. Zoom; a totally bizarre thought urged, "Yell cuss words!" when I sat in church listening to a talk on avoiding profanity. Kazowie; a rude thought tempted, "Spit in his food!" when I sat next to one of my dad's top clients at a formal banquet. These are examples of mild scary thoughts. I don't think it's necessary to share the darker, more extreme ones.

When the scary thoughts started shooting at me, I had no idea where they came from or what to do about them. I didn't dare talk about them with anyone because I feared people would think I was crazy or evil. Rather than seek help, I repressed them away deep in my mind, all the while feeling guilty and worried. I never acted on the thoughts. I just pretended they didn't exist.

Another symptom of my developing disorder was an addiction. Many people who have bipolar illness abuse drugs or alcohol to escape the agony of depression. I knew these were wrong. I became dependant on another "legal" substance. This substance had as much power on my mind and body as drugs or alcohol. It got me going in the morning and settled me down at night. It pumped me up when I exercised and helped improve my athletic performance. It enhanced my emotions in all my activities. During my teenage years it became an addiction that I invited in with, as Journey sang, "open arms." The substance was music.

I'm not saying the music was bad. I'm saying the beat, the harmonies, and the volume affected me profoundly. It literally had the same effect as amphetamines. Constantly listening to music enabled me to float above depression and blast out worry most of the time.

I want to point out something very important here. When you read my early mania and depression symptoms, you probably thought to yourself, "I have felt all of these at different times in my life. Do I have bipolar disorder?"

Don't worry. Not everyone who gets songs stuck in their head, who loses sleep because something is on their mind, or who makes grand plans for high achievement has bipolar disorder. Most people who have unpleasant or scary thoughts, who worry about silly things, who feels big guilt for small mistakes, or who sometimes feels the wrenching weight of depression pushing down in their gut do not have bipolar disorder.

Everyone experiences mild symptoms. Bipolar disorder is a chemical imbalance in the brain that physically forces untreated symptoms to the extreme. By living a simple, basic, healthy lifestyle of regular exercise, proper sleep, a good diet, and controlling stress, most people do not fall victim to extreme mania or lasting, deep depression.

As I grew into the later teenage years, my symptoms of mania and depression became more and more extreme. I didn't recognize or understand them. I never considered the possibility that the symptoms could be indicators of a developing mental illness.

Teenage years are like an amusement park ride. Everyone has highs and lows, but my roller coaster was about to shoot off the track. However, let's not let go of the safety bar, throw our hands over our head and yell "Weeeeee!" just yet. First, I must tell you about one other obsession. She was an "upper" that danced into my mind and heart in the mountains of Idaho. You guessed it. The summer before my senior year in high school, I fell in love.

The love story begins at a place called Badger Creek in Idaho. Though there were many thrilling activities during the day, I didn't go to the summer youth camp for dillydally daytime games. I had perfect plans for the fleeting free time-night time. The crisp and cool air brightened the stars as they illuminated the sage and aspen-covered mountains.

A lone boom box, sitting on the log next to the dimming campfire gently and softly strummed the loving strains of Def Leppard's "Love Bites." I know, I know. What kind of loony romantic would choose the hard-rock band, Def Leppard, in a setting like this? Well, that was the only tape I could find and at the time, I didn't care what song was playing. It could have been "Rock! Rock! 'Til You Drop!" and we still would have been slow dancing. All that mattered right then was that

I was with Dawn Fisher. We were alone in the night, under the stars, keeping warm by hugging close while dancing in the mountain dust.

Words were not needed to enhance the mood. As we danced in silence my thoughts waltzed around the two of us, and how our relationship had progressed to more than "just friends."

From the time we met earlier in the summer until the summer youth camp, we had seen more and more of each other. At first we happened to bump into each other at school functions, road races, or youth gatherings. After a while the meetings turned into, "Oh, you're here too, what a coincidence!" kind of meetings.

Every day, while training for cross-country, I always made it a point to run past her house or the ice cream parlor where she worked. I would leave a love note under the windshield wiper of her truck. After work she left notes on my basketball hoop pole. Needless to say, I did a lot of running, shot a lot of baskets, and ate a lot of starlight mint ice cream that summer.

When we learned of the summer youth camp, we each agreed to go and planned to secretly meet after curfew. Now, as I danced with her under the stars, I was convinced our love and commitment was mutual.

The next day on the bus ride home we sat next to each other holding hands in front of everyone. With headphones on my ears and Dawn stroking my hand, I closed my eyes in heavenly bliss and dreamed about how with Dawn as my girlfriend, my upcoming high school senior year, 1989, would be the best year of my life.

Chapter 3
Go Ski Wampus

As I think back on memories of the 1988-1989 school year I still feel a splash of excitement. It was the time of my prime in athletics, the time when I felt studlier than the Arabian stallion my parents had to keep two fences away from the mares. My high school senior year was the climax of my youth, the time of fearless fitness, coolest confidence, and frisky friendships.

At the beginning of that magical school year, I was honored to be elected a captain of the cross-country team. Our team wasn't typical. While other high schools begged and pleaded to get five or six athletes to come out on a regular basis, my high school cross-country team consistently ran in a pack of over 30 members. We placed high in the region and state meets.

In the winter, I didn't make the school hoops team so I enjoyed participating in church basketball instead. Winning the regional tournament and being voted our team's MVP felt great.

The most radical rush of the year came in the springtime when my school's track and field team won first place in the state tournament. I didn't qualify to run in the state meet, but my coaches and teammates convinced me that as one of the team captains, the victory was as much mine as anyone's.

The reason I share these achievements is not to boast. It is to show that people with developing mental illness are not always the quiet and mysterious "loners," as my friends and I used to call introverted young folks. It's not always the "weird guy" who draws demented art displays, or the computer geek who seems to be out of touch with the real world. Many who later develop mental illness are high achievers in their youth and early adulthood. They are the class presidents, the social butterflies, the blooming musicians with multiple scholarship offers, or the junior prom queens. Perhaps this is why it comes as such a shock to everyone when mental illness strikes.

That year, no matter what activity I participated in, I could always look to the stands and see Dawn, clapping and cheering my every success, and sending encouraging words with each defeat. She became my greatest motivation to achieve. Dawn had a saying she always used to tell me: "No matter where you finish in a race, or life, you will always be number one with me."

Her words were very soothing because I seldom finished with the super-high marks I expected in my grandiose, perfectionist plans. Dawn said she loved me despite my "failures." When I was with her, I always felt like a winner. Whenever I needed encouragement, a hug, or someone to mouth "olive juice" to me, she was there. What's olive juice? Mouth it in the mirror and see what it looks like you are saying.

Now the race through my senior year came around the corner. As I sprinted down the final stretch toward graduation, I knew great changes waited at the finish line. How I hoped my relationship with Dawn would continue to grow, but I could only guess what the future would bring. For the last assignment of the year in my college prep English class, the teacher had us write a letter to ourselves. This letter was to be sealed until May 25, 1999. Ten years seemed so far away, but I took the assignment seriously and wrote the following letter:

Dear Self,

Well today is the 25th of May, 1989, so it will be 1999 when you read this, and you will be 27 years old! Hey, old fogy! Who are you married to? How many kids? It better not be more than three! So did you graduate from college? Did you major in communications? I am really wondering where I will be as far as a job or career. How ever was your volunteer mission? Where ever did you go? It was probably some oriental language speaking one, eh? Chinese or something.

Are you still in touch with your high school buddies, most importantly, Dawn? How did it turn out? I wish I knew. I'm thinking about music now, here are some songs, do you remember them? Love Bites – Def Leppard, Journey – Open Arms, Endless Summer Nights – Richard Marx. Do these songs bring happy memories or sad ones? Oh I hope and pray they'll bring happy ones. If not, the girl you married is one awesome girl.

I just realized that 1999 is like a year away from 2000! Whoa, dude, you had better repent! The end is nigh! Actually, I know you'll still be close to Jesus. But always remember to choose the right.

Well, that's my advice from me as a teen. Stay close to God and be kind to the wife and kids! Don't forget the youth fire, and keep it alive! Take care, dude!

Just as my coaches put us through extremely difficult workouts in order to make us successful athletes, I figured the sacrifice and hard work of going on a volunteer mission would help me become a gold-medal father and husband. I wrote in the letter that I probably would be assigned to the Orient because in my mind it was the one place that would challenge me the most. It is kind of amazing and crazy the way my fears predicted exactly where I would go, but, then again, 1989 was crazy in its own way.

High school craze is healthy fun for most youth, but with the undetected illness building inside, for me it was the onramp to a freeway of mania. As I read the letter now, I can see quite clearly warning signs of conflict between outward confidence and inward doubt. At the time, however, I definitely didn't notice anything wrong. I was so intensely twitter pated, and always had the radio blasting so loudly, I drove right through the signs that warned, "Do Not Enter!" "Wrong Way!"

After high school graduation Dawn and I dated through the summer and often verbally expressed love for each other. I came to believe I succeeded in winning her heart forever. Mentally I needed her love desperately. Thoughts of Dawn's love lifted depression even more effectively than music or exercise. At the end of the summer, as darkness descended a little sooner each night, I knew our time together was quickly coming to a close.

On the last date of the summer, before she left for college in another state, I took her to our favorite spot–Wampus. Where's Wampus? Wampus was the name I had given a mountain slope to the east of my house. In the winter when the cold, crisp air offered pounds of precious powder and I couldn't afford a ski pass, I would go "ski Wampus."

As we sat on top of Wampus, we talked of how our relationship had grown. Before long we found ourselves knocking on the door of the future and the time of separation we faced while I was away on my mission. We both agreed that the mission I had chosen to serve was very important—even more important than our relationship at that time. We decided while I was away, I should focus my efforts and attention completely on my missionary work rather than on us, and she should date other guys. It wasn't the first time our lips touched, however, that night her tender kiss made me even more confident of her love and devotion. From then on I never considered that anything or anyone could come between us.

The next day Dawn left for school and I started the process of applying for my mission. In the mission service I signed up for, applicants didn't get to choose where in the world they would be sent. They could write in if they had previous foreign language training and if they would prefer to go to foreign or stateside missions, but when it came down to it, they really could be assigned to go anywhere. Not knowing where I would be sent made for a fun guessing game during the waiting period after sending in my mission application papers.

While waiting for my mission assignment many friends and family asked me where I wanted to go. My answer was always that I hoped to go to a Spanish-speaking mission. My reason was that my older brother, Cris, was on a mission in Argentina. I thought it would be fun to rap in Spanish with him after we both had returned home. I'm glad that no one ever asked me if there was anywhere I didn't want to go, because I was ashamed to admit that I feared Asian countries.

I grew up on a cherry farm where one year we hired Laotian immigrants to pick our cherries. As I wandered through the orchard, I listened to them talk. To my ears their language sounded like chatter. It seemed so foreign. I hardly believed they could understand each other.

The food they ate also seemed totally opposite of what I was used to. They often left behind whole fish skeletons! They had eaten the eyeballs, brains and everything. "How weird," I thought to myself.

With the strange foods and the chattery language, I felt that our differences were as vast as the ocean that separated our countries of origin. Fearing I would jinx myself by admitting the one place I didn't want to go, the only place I ever mentioned my fear of Asia was in the letter I wrote to myself to be opened ten years later.

Thinking of serving a mission in my own country also placed fear in my heart. "Stateside" missions, in my mind, tended to be dull and uneventful, and I feared the arrogance of my country's people would make it too easy to say, "Hit the road kid; don't bother me with your religious fanaticism!" I wanted excitement, adventure, and a place that would give me material for brilliant stories when I got home. I also wanted to go to a country where the people were humble and desirous for the message I brought.

So where was I called to serve? Big surprise; it was the Taiwan Taichung Mission. When I read the mission assignment, I remember thinking, "I'm going to go to that island, sit in a grass hut in the middle of a rice paddy, and read my Bible for two years. I'll never learn to speak Mandarin Chinese. Oh, well, at least it wasn't a stateside mission."

My dad sensed an urgent need for me to study the language, so he rushed to the store, bought a "learn to speak Mandarin" book and tape, and gave them to me. "You have to study the language," he encouraged.

I took the kit up to my room, turned off the tunes, and put in the language tape. It said, "Good morning Mr. Lee. Zao an Li Xian Sheng." Stunned at my complete lack of understanding, depression seeped into my stomach as fast as heartburn from a relish-covered hotdog. I turned off the tape, took it out, and put in a music tape with a relieving "tum, tum tum tum" beat.

I listened for a few moments but the song offered no comfort. I needed stronger medicine. There was only one place to find it. A good three-and-a-half hour drive separated Rexburg, where Dawn was going to school, and my home. But I didn't care; I had to see her. I called her up and told her I wanted to show her my mission assignment. Of course I didn't tell her I needed a lift out of depression. I made it sound as if I was coming up to personally share my good news. She sounded excited that I was coming, so I jumped in my family's Chevy Suburban and started my trek to Idaho.

The closer I got, the more excited I became. I envisioned Dawn running toward me for a twirling embrace. We'd hug and kiss and hold hands-just like we had on Wampus Mountain. Then she'd parade me around to all her new friends and tell them that this is the one she is always talking about. "He finally came and here he is: the greatest missionary ever sent to Taiwan!" Then she'd look at me with the proud look that says, "You'll always be number one with me."

The more I thought about it the higher my mood rose. Soon I was so caught up in the reunion that I forgot all about my real reason for going to see her. Little did I know I was headed for my first crash–no, not the Suburban I was driving–but my first crash from a manic high to severe depression. When I arrived, she did give me a hug, but it wasn't as enthusiastic as I had pictured. Yes, she did introduce me to her friends and roommates, but not with the words and passion I had anticipated. She did hold my hand, but just for a few minutes–and only in private. Looking back now I can see how my over-dependence on her love caused the onset of depression. At the time, I didn't have any idea what was happening, I only knew my heart was bleeding instead of pumping.

As I took it all in, an overwhelming feeling of sadness filled my whole body. It was as if someone poured wet concrete into my veins, packed clay around my eyes, and stacked rocks on my stomach. The more time passed, the more the concrete hardened. I hung my head. I dragged my feet. I didn't talk. I just slowly followed her from dorm to dorm. It was all I could do to keep from lying down, curling up into the fetal position, and bawling my eyes out.

Then came the ultimate killer. Dawn turned to me and quietly asked the stabbing words, "What's wrong, you look so down?"

I knew how to answer this question. "Oh, I'm just tired."

I waited for the comfort, the hug, the hand squeeze-anything. All she said was, "Oh, well I hope you're okay driving home."

Luckily, one of our mutual friends from high school was Dawn's roommate. She must have recognized somewhat the reason for my Dr. Jekyll-Mr. Hyde transformation. She came over and whispered, "Pull yourself together. You'll only make her less attracted to you, acting like that!"

Somehow, I found courage in her words and managed to perk up. By the time I was ready to leave, I was somewhat myself again. The whole incident happened in less than an hour's time. I felt it was so out of character for me that as I drove home I couldn't help but wonder exactly what had happened.

Hungry for an answer, I wondered and pondered as miles and miles of prolific potato fields flew past. But even after a good hour of thinking, my combo meal still remained short an order of fries. How could I fix something when I couldn't see the problem?

Finally, somewhere near the Idaho/Utah border I came to the conclusion that what had happened was Dawn's fault. I figured the only way to fix the problem was to convince her that she needed to love me better. How could I do this? Then, I came up with a promising plan. I decided to use my "missionary farewell" meeting in church to give her an inspired message. Although I knew many friends and family would attend the farewell, as I prepared my speech, my mind was focused entirely on Dawn.

Finally, the day of my farewell arrived. When it was my turn to speak, I stood up and carefully walked to the pulpit. Dawn and some of her friends had driven down from Idaho and were sitting below me in the front row. When I saw the smile on her face gleaming up at me, I took courage and began addressing the congregation.

To conclude my speech, I pulled a strategic and rather rash stunt. Everyone gasped when I reached down behind the pulpit, pulled up a boom box, and put it in front of the microphone. "Like my portable stereo system? I always have my music with me," I joked, as I pushed play and the tape began playing the introduction. When it came time to sing, I looked down into Dawns eyes and sang with all the emotion I could muster a song titled "Look to God and Live."

The music blended warmly with the gentle message. Many in the audience pulled out handkerchiefs. But the beauty of the song wasn't the reason for my smile and confidence. Rather, I performed with all my heart, trying to share a message with Dawn-that if she looked to God, He would give her whatever help she needed. How I desperately hoped God would make her aware how much I needed her!

Love is healthy. Dependence on another person to supply bushels of on-demand affection is not healthy. The only one with perfect love is God. I knew this, but I didn't accept it. I desired Dawn's love for me to be as perfect and grand as my Father in Heaven's.

As I sang and watched the look in her face, a world-record mile time wouldn't have matched the feeling of accomplishment that came over me. The tears in her eyes and the way she stared up at me convinced me that she understood and accepted the message. At the end of the

29

meeting, she ran over and gave me that blissful, swirling hug. Now, I was sure my message had made it through and I could focus entirely on my mission.

That evening before Dawn returned to Rexburg, there were two voices in my ears. The first was Dawn's gentle whisperings of, "I love you." With one final kiss goodbye, she slipped an envelope into my hand, got in her truck, and drove away. Then the other voice almost audibly taunted, "Two more days, and you're in the Orient for the next two years." I dashed to my room, threw on my headphones, and cranked up my favorite reggae group, UB40. The syncopated rhythms blasted out the voice of fear.

I sat on my bed bobbing to the music, thinking about my "many rivers to cross" for a few minutes before I realized that someone was sitting next to me. I looked up and saw my mother. I took off my headphones so I could hear her talk.

"You know the mission rules won't allow you to listen to that, don't you? Maybe you should start breaking away from it now."

Annoyed, I shot back, "I'll follow mission rules when I'm a missionary."

"It's your choice," she said with pain in her eyes.

I turned away from her gaze, put the headphones on, and tuned her out. She put her hand on my knee for a moment and then stood up to leave. I opened my eyes and watched her slowly walk out of the room.

I felt even more depressed. Then I remembered the envelope Dawn had slipped me. I took it out and ripped open the perfume-scented paper. Inside was a poem she had written. Tears filled my eyes as I read the final line, "God be with you 'til we meet again, my friend."

Chapter 4
Language Training

Before traveling to Taiwan I first needed to report to the Missionary Training Center in Provo, Utah. Because I needed foreign language as well as missionary skills training, my stay at the MTC would be for two months. My local church leader was scheduled to come to our house to give me a blessing and officially start my service as a full-time missionary at 8:30 on the eve of my entering the MTC.

That evening, as I packed my suitcases, I thought about the rules of my mission and the sacrifices they required: No kisses and hugs from Dawn, no full-court basketball games, no skiing (no snow for that matter), and no "worldly" music. Then I thought of the benefits: People will praise me and look up to me. I will help others find true happiness. I will be doing what God wants me to. I will gain personal growth that I could not get anywhere else. I will leave as a boy, and come back a man. Oh yes, there was also one other minor benefit that may have crossed my mind: Dawn wanted to marry a man who served an honorable mission. So, despite the sacrifices, I believed the rewards for going were well worth it.

Looking back now, I can see how blind I was to the depth of true sacrifice and the magnificent blessings to be gained from it. I was looking at the "right now." God was looking at the long term. He knew that character-molding suffering was just around the corner. He also knew that essential growth for eternal happiness was around the corner...and down the road. I thought I had signed up for a two-year trip to Taiwan. In reality I was beginning a journey down a road a lifetime in length.

As I finished packing, I looked at the clock. It said 8:25. I still had five more minutes. I stuck in a tape of my favorite group, Alphaville, and turned up "Forever Young." It was the song I had saved to be "the last one." Like an injection, the lyrics and harmonies of the song filled my mind and body.

As the song came to a close and before the trumpet duet could ring out "forever," someone tapped me on the shoulder. I looked up and saw my dad. When I took off the headphones, he quietly said, "He's here." I was so overcome by the moment that I forgot to turn the stereo off. All I could do was set the headphones on the bed, take a deep breath, and follow Dad downstairs.

I don't remember much about the meeting with my church leader. I remember he had a happy smile on his face and he spoke with sparkling enthusiasm. The only words I remember from his blessing were, "I bless you to learn the language quickly, that you will be able to speak so fluently, you will use it in a future career." After the blessing finished, I felt a little bit changed. I knew that now I was a full-time missionary. As quickly as the click of my stereo's automatic-off, my time of service had begun.

My family drove me to the MTC early the next morning. At the front door a bright and bubbly volunteer worker stuck a neon orange dot on my collar and whisked us away to a big room full of other orange-dot-bearing missionaries, their families and friends. I knew what to expect in that room. My brother Cris and other missionary friends gave me plenty of warning. It was the "Moses" room as they called it-or in other words, the "parting of the missionaries" room.

First, they showed a short video that, among other things, talked about how many thousands of pounds of Captain Crunch cereal the missionaries ate each week at the MTC. After the video, the MTC president stood up. Even though I knew about the "parting" part that followed his speech, somehow I found the ability to listen to what he said. He spoke of "the Spirit."

"Missionaries with a desire to serve God, who follow the rules, and work hard can obtain the Spirit," he said. "The Spirit is what makes successful missionary work possible. Without it, others will not believe the message they share. With it, the sky is the limit to what they can do." Oh yeah, that limitless sky-the same cliché I had heard in pep talks back in my high school track days.

The rest of his talk faded as I dreamed of following every mission rule 100%, working harder than any other missionary, and having the Spirit so strongly, I could soar in the limitless sky. I wonder if the MTC president spoke of the simple humility and frequent repentance that can invite the Spirit back when a missionary inevitably falls short of the mark. Maybe he spoke of setting reasonable and attainable goals, and measuring success by personal improvement and dedication-not by being the best when compared to others.

"We'll give you five minutes to say good bye to your family and friends, then will the missionaries please go through this door and the families go out this other door." It was time for the parting of the missionaries. This loaded conclusion to the MTC President's talk shot me out of the sky and blasted onion peelings into the congregation's eyes. As soon as he finished speaking, almost everyone simultaneously burst into tears. Having been forewarned, I was one of the few who held them in. I quickly hugged my family and darted for the door.

Once I made it through the door, the onion peel effect immediately vanished behind a sizzling aura of excitement and enthusiasm. Outside the "missionary door" the MTC boiled over with enticing and tasty morsels of that "Spirit" the president had spoken of. First I came to a set of lines. At the front of the lines I received my new nametag. I held it in my hand staring in disbelief. At the top, the Roman characters spelling out my name in English were easy to read. Under my name a series of Chinese characters looked like art made from chicken scratches. "That is so cool!" I blurted out. Then the thought came to me, "Pretty soon, you will be able to read and understand what the characters mean!"

In the next line, they handed out books and supplies. I couldn't fathom how I would use three huge bottles of vitamins and would have passed by them, but looking at my tag, a volunteer smiled, tucked the bottles in my bag and said, "Hang on to these. You may need them to supplement your diet where you're going."

I took the vitamins to Taiwan, but never took them into my diet. They could have been a tremendous help. Later on, I will write in detail how poor eating became a big contributor to my first breakdown. For now I'll just say, a regular, well balanced diet would be much, much higher on my list of priorities if I could go back and relive my mission experience.

In the last line, I picked up my Mandarin language book, other training materials, and a map of the MTC dorms. Then, completely loaded with supplies and plenty of compliments of how sharp I looked with my flashy nametag, I decided to go find my new sleeping quarters.

As I carried the bags of supplies, I remembered my luggage and thought, "I'll have to go back to get my suitcases." Just as I reached the room, in bounced my new family. Their hands carried my suitcases and their faces radiated smiles and cheer. "We got these for you!" one said thrusting his hand out in pure missionary style. "You can take that orange dork dot off your collar now. I stuck mine behind my tag for memory's sake. By the way, I'm Ken Bown, your new companion, and these are our roommates, Jon and Tom. Now we're all here; let's go get some grub." Their cheery moods lifted my spirits even higher. With light hearts and hungry stomachs we skipped away to the cafeteria.

After dinner we hurried to our evening class. We found our names listed on the classroom door with eight other missionaries. All of us had been assigned to the Taiwan Taichung mission. When our teacher came in he told us how lucky we were to get to go to Asia. "The people are awesome and you're going to fall in love with them. They are kind, polite, and generous. The Orient is the greatest place in the world to serve a mission!"

Then he said something that permanently influenced my attitude about learning Chinese. He said, "Anyone can learn Chinese. I am just an average Joe and I learned it. If I can do it, you can too." From that point forward I never feared the language again.

The high from that first day lasted for a few days. But all too soon, life in the MTC deflated into a regular routine. I noticed the MTC workers weren't always as chipper as they had been that first day. Other missionaries had open disagreements in the gym and shower areas. Even the teachers looked a little tired on occasion.

Life in the MTC was good, but it wasn't as perfect as it had seemed. The same was true of myself. After a few days, I found it impossible to maintain an optimistic attitude, to remember all that was thrown at me in class, and to be as spiritual all the time as I thought I should be.

Withdrawal from my medicine (music and Dawn) made it harder to mask the depression that weighed me down. One experience openly exposed these hidden feelings. I call it the "Sven" incident.

Our leaders encouraged us to write friends back at home who were not believers and invite them to learn more about Christ. Growing up, nearly all of my friends came from good Christian families. Sven was a foreign exchange student who ran track with me. When I dashed through my mental list of candidates (which I could count on one hand), his name finished at the top.

With high hopes of his quick conversion, I sent him a letter. A few days later I received his reply. My heart pounded and hands shook like I had just run a track event as I read the letter. First he thanked me for writing and then told me the latest news about the track team.

He said the team was doing well but they missed me. He also told me about some happenings with our common friends. His words were like happy hurdles as I sprinted toward the anticipated answer to my invitation to learn more about my religion. When it came, the words stuck me like a javelin thrown astray just before I crossed the finish line. My heart bled as I read, "I appreciate what you're trying to accomplish on your mission, but leave me out of your plans. I'm not interested in joining your church. Please don't write me about it anymore."

I tried to be brave and positive, to think of how I could "get up and finish the race." But, the blow and sinking feeling of rejection weighed on me all through my afternoon class. I couldn't come to any conclusion as to what went wrong and why I had failed. The words of Sven's letter and my imaginary conversations with him rolled around over and over in my head like a forgotten egg roll on one of those gas station turny, rolly, warming machines. The more I thought about it, the more I could feel the heat of depression splitting open my emotions. At dinnertime, when the rest of the missionaries left the classroom, I told Ken I needed to be alone for a minute. He quietly walked out of the room and shut the door.

I fell to my knees as the tears boiled over. "Please spare Sven," I pleaded in prayer. "He doesn't know what he is rejecting. I tried my best but..." On and on I prayed, begging for forgiveness of my unworthiness and pleading for Sven to change his mind. Ken must have heard my sniffling because, when I finally finished my prayer, he was standing over me.

I stood up and between sniffles told him about the "terrible" letter. He replied with the comforting words, "Maybe the time isn't right, and at least he is still your friend. All hope isn't lost. You just need to give him time."

We talked about it for a while and I was able to stop crying. Still, from that point forward, depression became a smoldering ember inside that egg roll cooker that flared and flamed every time gusts of guilt blew. There were one or two times that I didn't wake up on time. There were a few instances when I spoke English when I was supposed to speak only Chinese. I talked about skiing Wampus during study time here, and arrived at class late because I stayed too long playing basketball in the gym there.

Ken didn't know it, but he was actually in a trio. My other companion was depression. At one point I recorded in my journal, "perhaps I have inherited Mother's depression." Sadly, my reaction to this realization was one of denial and ignorance.

I wouldn't allow the thought that I may need medication and counseling. Instead I made myself believe sin was the reason for my depression. I thought obtaining forgiveness and then living perfectly was the key I needed to start my car and get me rolling down the freeway of mental bliss. It was another apple slice in the ignition thing. The real "key" I needed was to seek help for depression. Instead, I kept shoving apple slices in the ignition by falling to my knees and begging for forgiveness each time depression struck.

Seeking forgiveness is a great and necessary thing to allow happiness back into our lives. For all my small mistakes, I'm sure forgiveness came. However, with all my repentance, the depression still didn't depart. Sin was not the main reason for the recurrent dark and gloomy feelings; it was a chemical imbalance in my head. What I really needed was medication and education.

I kept all this repentance and perfectionism inside. Except for crying over Sven, my symptoms were a hidden, inner and mostly subconscious struggle. On the outside, my actions, appearance, and speech reflected how I thought I was supposed to be: positive, happy, and diligent-all the time. In other words, on the outside I was dynamite, on the inside a smoldering flame.

I went into the MTC undiagnosed and ignorant of my mental health. I knew mission life would be different, but I didn't realize how the high standards and strict rules, combined with my perfectionist and grandiose thinking could cause such an enormous amount of mental pressure. I had taken missionary preparation classes that taught about preparing physically and spiritually. Now I know that mental preparation is just as important.

But it isn't just missionaries who need to be aware of their mental health condition. Late teenage and early twenties are a time of great change in most people's lives. It's when students leave home (often for the first time) for college. During those early 20's a lot of folks choose to get married. It's also around those years that most people leave the nest to spread their own wings and try to soar into a new career. So, what does this have to do with bipolar disorder? Most mental breakdowns happen just after teenage years during times of high stress and major lifestyle changes.

As you read my story, keep in mind that the mission I was serving wasn't necessarily the cause of the mental breakdowns; it was a chemical imbalance in my body. The pressures of university expectations, challenges in a marriage, raising children, making ends meet, or any other major lifestyle change also could have sparked the same type of breakdown had I not volunteered for a mission.

I hope I don't give the impression my entire MTC experience was cloud-skipping bliss on the outside and stone-sinking discouragement on the inside. It wasn't always that way. My time in the MTC was like water skiing on slow-moving water. The river of guilt and depression constantly pulled down on my mood and clouded my vision of self-worth. However, a powerful motorboat driven by genuine people continually pulled me forward on a thrilling ride. Every time I fell, these wonderful friends always circled back to pick me up before I could be washed away. Now, as I look back on that MTC adventure, I remember the crashes but haven't forgotten many special experiences and times of genuine joy.

Of all the wonderful memories in the MTC, the greatest was the return of my big brother Cris. He returned home after I had been in the MTC for just over a month. Obviously, I hadn't seen him in two years. Knowing he was home, I thought about him a lot. I knew the MTC had strict rules against having visitors. The standard was set to help new missionaries focus entirely on their important work. I had heard the joke that the only difference between the MTC and a jail was that they allow visitors at the jail. Nonetheless, I hoped for a chance to see him.

Journal Entry 11-17-1990 MTC, Provo, Utah

Yesterday we got up, showered, ate breakfast and walked to the MTC's special training facility just east of our dorms. Since we are only allowed to go there once a week to receive the specialized training it's always a nice break from our normal routine. After our training session, as Ken and I were walking out the doors to head back to the MTC dorms, I glanced over to the waiting room at the entrance of the building. I couldn't believe what I saw. Sitting there smiling at me was my beloved brother, Cris! He had gotten special permission to go there and see me. What a grand reunion. He looked so good. In our short time together we talked about a lot of spiritual things, mainly missions. It was great and I learned a lot. I feel more prepared to hit the field. I also got a different perspective about missions. He told me that it's not so serious of a deal that we shouldn't ever smile and we should remember to relax now and then. Now I don't look back, just ahead to live this two years the best I can because when it's over, it's over and I'll be back to the normal life. I love that man. I'm so grateful for him.

Seeing Cris chased away my depression and I charged into the remainder of my MTC stay with new enthusiasm. The fresh energy was good but it also powered new grandiose plans. Two weeks before our departure date, new Mandarin speaking missionaries arrived at the MTC. Friendships formed quickly. During our few moments of free time just before bed a few of us found ourselves talking about some pretty deep, spiritual stuff with one of the new missionaries. He had a book that outlined steps to "having your calling and election made sure."

Being raised in a very religious home, I thought it strange that I had never heard this phrase before. My memory of the way the new missionary explained it, was that having your calling and election made sure meant you believe so strongly, you pass the trial of your faith, and Jesus Christ Himself appears to you, forgives your sins, and secures your place in His kingdom.

Just like Moses at the burning bush, when the Lord told him to take off his shoes, we didn't understand the ground we were walking on was extremely sacred. It was stimulating to talk about, but we confused our excitement with spirituality.

As I heard the other missionaries talk about how not just prophets, but common people like us have had this happen, you can guess what my new grandiose plan became? Actually, that was the third super-goal of my mission up until then.

Before I entered the MTC, I made a goal to work out every day and build my vertical jump high enough to dunk a basketball with two hands behind my head. I figured two years was plenty of time to do it. At the time I went into the MTC, the biggest thing I had slam-dunked was a volleyball-and with just one hand. I could jump up and grab the rim with one hand just about every time but never found the ability to dunk a basketball. I was five feet, eleven inches tall. To dunk a basketball with two hands behind my head, I would need a vertical leap of over 40 inches. So, that exceedingly high goal was the first piece of extra luggage that I packed for my mission.

I acquired my next piece of heavy baggage when another missionary told me of a "great" idea. He said if I memorized just a few verses a day by the end of my mission I could have the whole Bible memorized! So, each morning I tried to memorize the number of versus he had calculated. Don't forget on top of that memorization, I crammed in ten hours of Mandarin every day as well.

So, according to my plans, at the end of my mission when I arrived back on American soil, I would leap from the plane with over 18 inches of improvement in my vertical jump, be able to rattle off hundreds of pages of memorized scripture, and have developed enough faith that my Savior personally descended down from heaven just to see me and secure my spot in His kingdom. I'll pause for you to chuckle and shake your head.

After a few days failing to memorize the scriptures, I got so far behind I quickly realized how impossible that goal was. So, I changed my goal from memorizing the Bible to reading it all the way through. There was a small catch around this goal that still kept it just out of my reach. I wanted to read the entire book by the end of mission–in Chinese. I heard that only a few Mandarin-speaking missionaries with the best language mastery did it. I wanted to be in that elite group.

Deep inside I must have known my goals were lavishly lofty because I chose never to tell anyone about them. I think I feared someone would tell me I couldn't achieve them. I wonder how I would have reacted if someone told me these extreme goals were indicators of a developing mental illness. Would I have had the humility to listen and try to change my thinking? Would I have been able to lower my self-expectations and set goals that revealed a person with weakness and limitations?

I don't think I could have. I kept my goals locked up in my mind, secretly believing and hoping they were possible. I wrote them down on a small three-by-five card in code so, if someone did see them, they wouldn't know what they meant. The first code was "2 hand slam BH" (two hand slam behind the head), the second was "Bible," and the third was "C&EMS" (Calling and Election Made Sure). I used the card as a bookmark for my scriptures so I would see the goals often.

With these hefty goals tightly tucked in my carry-on, I shouldered my portly pack and boarded the bus bound for the airport where my family anxiously waited to say hello and goodbye all over again. Seeing them after the long two months in the MTC felt good, but by this time I was ready to get on with my mission. Despite my bouts with depression, the MTC had pumped me up like an over-inflated helium balloon. Now I was yanking on my string, wanting to fly. After many hugs, a few pictures, and a farewell song in Chinese, we boarded the plane and then lifted off.

Chapter 5
Early Taiwan

Dear Dawn,

I can't believe I'm half a world away in Taiwan! Our mission president is here but his assistants are late driving the van to the airport to pick us up. I thought I'd use the time to write you a quick note.

On the flight over, I sat between two Asian men. The guy on my right was a businessman from Indonesia. He spoke English very well and seemed to be entertained by talking with me. As I told him about my missionary calling to the people of Taiwan, he told me that the Chinese people were very "keqi" or polite on the outside, but the secret was to figure out how they really felt in their hearts.

The guy on my left was a Taiwanese man who didn't speak any English. It was great fun speaking to him in my MTC Chinese. We actually communicated! It was quite educational conversing with the two personalities. Funny, but through the whole flight, they barely acknowledged each other.

As we descended over Taipei, I looked down at the lights, the streets, the traffic and the nighttime scenery. I thought to myself, "It looks just like home." Since we have gotten off the plane, passed through customs, picked up our luggage, and now are waiting here at the front entryway, however, I am quickly realizing that I am a long way from home. Many sights, smells, and sounds are quite different than anything I have ever experienced.

Still, as I write this, I am gaining a small and subtle sense of belonging. There's a big-screen TV just across the room that is playing music videos. Of course it's all in Chinese and though I can't understand the words, I do understand the message of the song. The man is alone, thinking of his loved one and wishing she could be with him. When I look a little closer, I can see where he spilled olive juice on his shirt.

Well, it looks like there is a van with a couple of anxious Americans driving up to the curb. They must be the APs (assistants to the president). Gotta run.

Love always, Andy.

So there I was: a missionary in Taiwan. As we began the long drive south from the airport headed for the city of Taichung, a misty rain darkened even more the dwindling twilight. Soon, dancing silver droplets were all I could see on the van's shaded windows. The solemn sound of windshield wipers seemed to swish away all conversation. Before long, jet lag carried the other missionaries away to worlds of silent snoozing. My exhausted body begged to drift away with them, but the obsessive storms in my manic mind wouldn't allow it.

Like random lightning strikes, thoughts flashed through my mind: "I can't believe I'm really in Taiwan! I'm on my mission! I've got to learn Chinese fluently! I wonder what my trainer will be like. I hope he is cool about working hard and following all the rules. I need to remember to get up early so I can work on my vertical jump. I missed working out the last three days in the MTC. I need to start learning Chinese characters so I can get going on my "read the Bible goal...."

The downpour didn't let up until we arrived in Taichung and entered the shelter of the mission home. There, the comfort of a soft mattress, warm blanket and cool pillow calmed my clouded mind and stilled the stifling storm.

The sun rose early the next morning. By the time I got up, piddly puddles were all that was left of the previous night's raging rain. I watched swarms of mosquito-like motor scooters splash through puddles on the busy street outside. "Hey, look at that!" I called to Ken, who appeared at my side. "There are five people on that one motor scooter! Two kids standing on the foot rest, a lady driving, and two kids sitting in back!" We watched a moment longer.

"Look, that one has six people on it and a dog in the front basket!" exclaimed Ken.

"They're moms taking kids to school. You'll get used to seeing that every day." We turned around to see Devon, one of the assistants who picked us up the night before. "We're going out for breakfast," he continued. "Everyone needs to be up, showered, dressed in missionary attire, and ready to go in one hour."

Emerging outside, moving away from the shelter of the mission home felt like being born into a new world. We followed Devon down the street toward a "zao dian" as he called the breakfast shop. I clung to him like the young foals back home used to stick close to their mothers when we took them for a ride away from the barn. Like the young foals I was curious of every new sight, sound and smell.

First, we came to a group of taxi drivers crouched Chinese style (with their heels flat on the ground and arms wrapped around their knees) in a circle under the shade of a palm-looking tree I later learned was a binlang (beetle nut) tree. I slowed down as we walked passed so I could listen closely to their conversation. I thought I would be able to catch something they said, but their words didn't sound like anything we had studied in the MTC. "How do you do?" they called out to us, their happy smiles flaring a bright red outline around their teeth. The MTC teachers told us about the ugly red stains that came from chewing binlang seeds. They said it was a lot like American chewing tobacco. I waved and then hurried to catch up with Devon.

"Could you understand what they were saying?" I questioned.

"Nope," he replied. "They were speaking in Taiyu."

"What's Taiyu?" I asked.

"Taiwanese," he answered. "Here in Taiwan there are many different dialects of Chinese that come from dalu, I mean mainland China. Mandarin is actually the Beijing dialect. Taiwanese is a dialect stemming mainly from the Fujian province. Down here in the south, Taiyu is very common. It's the informal language that many of them use when they hang out. It's kind of like when we speak in slang with our buds in America, but Taiyu is a complete language."

Nobody seemed to notice that I stopped walking, opened up my scriptures and scribbled something on the bookmark. I'm sure Devon would have been quite amused if he had known that I was writing my newest grandiose goal: "Taiyu." As if Mandarin wasn't enough, I set a goal to learn to speak fluent Taiwanese while on my mission as well.

As we entered the lively breakfast shop, Devon pointed up at a big board on the wall with vertical (up and down that is) lines of different colored Chinese characters written with felt tip markers. "What do you want to eat?" Devon kidded, knowing that we couldn't read the menu or even know what the food was called. Pretending to misunderstand our babbling reactions, he teased further, "Oh, yeah, I forgot you can't read characters yet. Here, I'll read the menu for you: danbing, roubao, youtiao. To drink you can have bing doejiang or ri de." He and a few of the others laughed, but I didn't think it was funny. It wasn't that being the brunt of his joke was bad, I just hated being in the shadowy side of a language barrier.

Devon must have seen the scowl on my face because he came over, put his arm around me and said, "Don't worry, Andy. The language will come with time, but remember, you don't need perfect language to communicate and influence people for good.

After breakfast, Devon hurried us back to the mission headquarters for an important meeting. We were all excited because the mission president was going to give us our assigned areas and the names of our new companions/trainers. President Watson knew how to keep our attention, because he put that information at the end of the agenda.

The first item he spoke on was the mission's program for learning the language. He felt memorizing the six discussions missionaries used to introduce the basic beliefs was the most effective and important language-acquisition method. Bei ke (memorizing the discussions), as he called it, was the first and most critical level of the program. We weren't allowed to move to the second level or third level until we had passed off all six discussions. "That means I won't be able to start working on my goal of reading the Chinese Bible until I get to the third level!" I thought to myself, with much anxiety.

President Watson concluded by telling us the names of the missionaries who set the records for memorizing the discussions the fastest. "So-and-so missionary has the record for passing them off the soonest. He did it the first day he was on the island because he memorized all six discussions in the MTC. So-and-so missionary memorized all the discussions in two weeks after he got on the island."

"Wow!" I thought, remembering the MTC and how it took me a whole month to just be able to translate the first discussion. President Watson continued, "Most missionaries who really try, do it in three or four months." I took that as a challenge and set a goal to do it in one month (yet another grandiose goal).

The next thing that the president said was totally unexpected. "I don't want to embarrass Devon, but I would like to tell you about him. Devon struggled with the language at first. He didn't pick it up as quickly as the others who came on island with him did, but he continued studying and didn't get discouraged. After he memorized the discussions, he worked just as hard on the second and third levels. Many missionaries who reach that point stop working on their language. Through his whole mission, Devon has continued to study and learn. Now, he has become one of the best language speakers in our mission. Not only has he mastered the language, but he also teaches over 15 discussions a week and has baptized many converts who are now strong members. If you want an example of the way a missionary should be, you should look to Devon."

If this was a shot at a motivational speech, the president couldn't have hit my bull's eye more perfectly. When I saw that type of praise and perceived the honor flowing to Devon from the top of the totem pole, I recommitted to push myself harder than ever before. I would not settle for anything less than perfection.

I'd like to make a comment here for future leaders who try to motivate or coach youth. I think most young folks need pep talks, strong persuasion, and sometimes, even a kick in the behind to help them achieve their potential.

There are a few, however, who constantly kick themselves. What they really need is for a leader they regard highly to quietly take them aside and tell them they are doing enough. The words, "You're working as hard as you can. It's okay for you to take time to relax. Your personal health is more important than being the best," may be just as motivational to them as "Go, go, go! More, more, more! Work harder, harder, harder!" is to others. It's a difficult call to determine who needs what kind of encouragement. However, it's a call that may help prevent mental illness explosions.

Leaving the mission home to go to my first area, I felt fired up more than ever. The burning desire for high achievement was both good and bad: good because it motivated me to excel in my missionary efforts, bad because it ignited the fuse leading to my mental detonation. Happily, God made my fuse long enough to last ten more months.

How I treasure the memories of life-changing experiences while living on Formosa for that short time.

My first assignment was in the city Tainan with a colorful companion and talented trainer named Andre. From the moment he picked me up at the train station, sat me on the rack on the back of his bike, and pedaled toward our apartment, I knew this guy was special.

If you've ever been to Taiwan, you know the chaotic scene of the treacherous traffic. Zippy motor scooters, compact cars, and mammoth trucks buzzed, beeped, and bellowed all around us. As he confidently and cautiously pumped the pedals, Andre calmed and comforted my mind with happy humor.

"On the left you'll see the best zao dian (breakfast shop) in the city. Their doujiang (soy milk) is like nectar and their danbings (egg dumplings) are like manna. On the right you will see the daxue (university). Many golden contacts have been made there and we are teaching two awesome students there." His funny voice and happy tone transformed my fear into excitement. By the time we reached a street lined on both sides with towering apartment complexes, I felt as if we had arrived at home.

That night, after dinner we started our missionary work together. Not having anything scheduled, Andre said we would go and introduce ourselves to the people living in a nearby apartment complex and try to set up some teaching appointments. After locking our bikes up outside a huge apartment complex, we knocked on several doors.

At first, when people answered, Andre did all the talking. Just as I was getting comfortable he turned and said, "You get to talk to the next family." Determined to succeed at all costs I marched up to the next door and knocked. When a friendly man answered, I mustered up all my courage and recited my memorized introduction. The man smiled and said something I didn't understand. I could tell he was declining because he shook his head and stepped back to shut the door. As we walked away, Andre said I did great. I didn't think so. I was ashamed and humiliated that I couldn't understand the rejection.

Looking back at the struggles I had while learning the language, I wish I could have just shrugged them off with a smile and a chuckle. At the time, however, I wouldn't laugh or joke around about my mess ups. I didn't think they were funny. I couldn't accept that making mistakes was permitted and even expected.

I didn't know it, but my real problem actually had nothing to do with language. The thing that was shooting me down was unrealistic perfectionism. With the self-destructive mindset that I had to be perfect in order to feel good, more language mistakes and other human happenings launched explosive depression torpedoes into my mind and heart.

As I tried to stay afloat in the tumultuous sea of perfectionism, thanks to Andre, I never sank over my head. His light and quirky humor had a way of constantly buoying me up. Perhaps this fun-loving personality even helped to prevent a mental breakdown.

It happened one evening when we had about an hour or so of free time and decided to do some person to person contacting. There was a strip of shops close to where we were. We jumped on our bikes and rode over to them. We hadn't been there long when a dirty, deranged and drunk man staggered toward us. He knew we were Americans because he tried to speak English. All he could say was, "Help me, my family." He said it over and over.

I didn't know how to handle the situation. I worried he had a serious problem. I felt it was my duty to find out what it was, and then solve it for him. I tried to talk to him, asking, "Where is your family? What's wrong?" But, he didn't understand my English.

He just repeated again, "Help me, my family." I tried to talk to him in Chinese but he wouldn't answer that either. As Andre and I stood there, the man kept inching closer and closer. We kept backing up. He was so close it was all we could do to keep from gagging on his horrible breath. It smelled like a mixture of alcohol and thrush. What's thrush? It's a potentially crippling condition when a horse stands in wet manure so long that its hooves start to decay. As you can imagine, the smell is unforgettably rank.

As we continued to back up, I kept trying to talk to him. However, the more I talked, the closer he got, and the more scared and anxious I became. I was afraid that leaving him would be a sin for which I would be held accountable. I felt like a trapped animal. Just as my fear started turning to panic, to my great relief, Andre took charge. He stuck his hand out and stopped the man's advance. Then, looking him straight in the eyes, Andre said, in English, "Do you know what you need? Colgate."

"Colgate?" The man replied, obviously with no clue what it meant.

"Yes, Colgate. Colgate will fix your problem," Andre stated coolly.

You know how you get sometimes when you're really scared or freaked out and you just start laughing? That's what happened to me. The sarcastic yet serious look on Andre's face, the interest in the drunk's eyes and the release of panic all set me laughing uncontrollably. I tried to keep it in, but couldn't. As I laughed, Andre lost the ability to fake sincerity and also started laughing. When the man saw us laughing, he started laughing too!

We all stood there laughing for a minute. Then Andre turned to me and said, "Let's get out of here." He pushed the man aside and quickly unlocked our bikes. We hopped on and rode away, leaving the man behind, still standing there–laughing.

A few days later, while swimming in my sea of perfectionism, another huge wave crashed over me. We were riding our bikes home one night and passed the scene of an accident. When we passed by a policeman who was directing traffic I glanced over and saw a dead man lying face down on the pavement in a pool of blood!

The rest of the ride home, I tried to catch up to Andre. But, he rode so fast that I didn't reach him until we stopped in front of our apartment. As we locked our bikes up I said to him, "Wasn't that weird?"

He slowly looked up and said, "It was very sad." His bloodshot eyes and trembling lips showed that he had been crying all the way home.

That night as I lay in bed thinking about the experience and Andre's reaction, I realized just how much love he had for the people of Taiwan. Turning my thoughts inward, I examined my own reaction and came to the painful conclusion that my heart was completely numb. I didn't feel anything. I hadn't felt sorrow for the unfortunate man or given thought to his pitiable family. Following the experience, my only emotion was a feeling of strangeness.

I had heard that the best missionaries loved the people they served with all their heart. Guilt flooded my mind. Was I not a good missionary? Was I not working hard enough? Why couldn't I love these people like I should?

Something that could have helped me stay afloat at that difficult time was patience. If I could go back, I would grab that mental life preserver and allow myself time to become the missionary I wanted to be. I would not expect it the moment I arrived. I wish I could have known that just like homesickness, culture shock was a natural thing and I wasn't a bad or unworthy missionary because I experienced it.

Waves. Downs and ups like a buoy in a white-capped ocean. Every time my emotions rose up and I could see the magnificent view, something always pulled me back down. By this time, the word depression was a part of my vocabulary-in Chinese and English. But, I still had no idea that it was chronic depression that weighed me down each day. Rather, I thought it was normal missionary emotions that just needed a spiritual lift. My journal is full of entries that talk about wonderful experiences pulling me up from nagging depression. The following is a typical entry from that time in my mission:

12/1990 Tainan, Taiwan
Sunday, good day! Oh hurray, I had two things happen that helped me get out of the dumps. First, we were with Ronald, a young 13-year-old boy, teaching the third discussion. Before today, Ronald hadn't been impressed with anything we had tried to teach him. Today, however, after the discussion he suddenly said, "Wo xiangxin nimen (I believe what you're saying)." It was so awesome. I know now why Satan has been working so hard to bring me down these last few days. I forgot a valuable lesson that they said in the MTC: "When you're feeling the most down, it's because something great and wonderful is coming up." I need to remember to fight being down with everything I have, because success is right around the corner.

The second awesome thing happened when we were shanging ke ("Chinglish" for "teaching discussions") with a man who had a lot of questions. See, his parents and family all are Buddhist, so he has been taught Buddhist theory all his life. He didn't know if there was one God or a lot of them, what God was like, and a lot of other stuff. The lesson I learned was this: when I put myself in their shoes and really look at it from their point of view, and really want to help them, that's when the depression leaves and the peace sets in. I think I can sum it up with one word-empathy. If I have empathy, all the selfish feelings and self-pity leave. Empathy is the key. If I'm sad and depressed it's probably a selfish reason or excess temptation and pressure because Satan knows a good thing is about to happen. I need to fight Satan by remembering that success is coming.

Because I constantly spoke, thought, and taught about God and spiritual things, it was natural for me to assume that the downs came from the devil and the highs came from God. It made me think that if I were a better person, with better empathy, more faith, less selfishness, less self-pity, then God would lift me out of the pit of dark and seemingly ominous depression. Confused and convinced that working harder and being better would change my storms to sunshine I continued pressing forward forcing a smile on the outside and trying to understand why I felt down most of the time on the inside.

Many successes with Andre pulled my spirits up again and again. In the short two months I spent with him, we enjoyed meeting, teaching, and even baptizing many wonderful people. Although I couldn't see it, the growth I desired from serving a mission had begun.

When transfers came and I received word I was moving to the city, Kaohsiung, to be companions with a missionary from Japan, a splendid excitement filled my heart. "Perhaps being with him can help me to not only learn the language better, but also help me to love the people more," I thought.

Chapter 6
Yuan Fen

Journal Entry, 3-17-91, Kaohsiung, Taiwan.
Since I've been in Kaohsiung, I've started doing some serious heartfelt thinking. It started when we had a ke (discussion) with a guy who asked us, "How do you know the Holy Ghost has a unique personality and isn't just a robot from God?" Then last night we had a three hour ke with a different guy talking about whether bugs have a god and if there are animals in heaven. The questions didn't bother me, but the thing that sparked my thinking was the fact that I myself have never even thought of questions like that. All my life up till now I've always just accepted religious concepts. Mom said there was a God, so I believed. She said there was a Christ; I believed. All these people are searching, they think and wonder, and so I tell them, "Yeah, it's so easy. You just have to have faith, pray and read the scriptures, then you'll get your answers." It's the same answer that I've heard since I could talk. But now I'm questioning the same things whereas before I just accepted it all as truth.

Now that I'm away from the shelter of my parents, I've really started thinking about my own personal feelings and I find myself basically in the same situation as the people I'm teaching. Here I am, Mr. Missionary, telling them, "I know this is true." But inside I'm really thinking, "Do you really?" The church leaders all say that if you say it's true, then you will know it is. So I say it's true, and sometimes I really believe that I know it's true. But other times I wonder.

To me, logically the existence of God makes sense. That's way different from most people. Most people, we tell them, "Open your heart and close your mind." But to me it's like, close your heart and open your mind. I want to think about this and then look at my heart. It's like, what is this thing called faith? What is death like? What will it be like to live forever in the next life? Not the standard answer: well, our spirits leave our bodies and go to the spirit world and then we're resurrected and then judged and then because I've been good I can go to heaven and live forever, and then I don't think about it because, "after that we just don't know."

I really am wondering, what is reality right now? It's like, well I live to be happy. Before my mission I found happiness doing fun things like playing basketball, running, skiing, fishing, and listening to music. Now as a missionary I live for P-day ("preparation" day was one day a week when we got to take a day off from missionary work) when I can relax, play ball and just not think about these "serious" issues. I never talk about these things because people would think I'm a freak! You don't ask that kind of stuff. You just talk about the weather, sports, school and girls.

It feels like my life up until now has been pretty shallow. My motto has been: just live for the fun times, and like Dawn and I always said, "don't mess," or don't get into trouble because you need to be prepared for what happens in the next life-even though we don't know what it is like. I really feel like if I could get the full picture of eternity or at least the reality of it, then I wouldn't have to shrug off deep questions that I used to lay in bed at night and think about to the point of tears because I couldn't grasp it, so I'd go crying into Mom and Dad's room and they would say, "we just don't know, we have to wait till we die to find those things out. Right now, follow the commandments and don't worry about it." So I learned to shrug it off when I'd think about stuff like that. I'd fill my mind with temporary things—the next basketball game, the next track meet, the next date, and I just crowded out those deep-in-the-abyss thoughts.

Well, here I am thinking the same thoughts again but now deeper because I realize much more and have seen much more. I watch other people and I feel like I know how to read them. I can look at people and right away see their strengths and weaknesses. I can read most personalities pretty accurately and can guess where they have been and where they are going in life. But I'm finding the one person I can't read is this one. It's so easy for me to see others, but I have no clue about myself. Why am I here in Taiwan? What is the Lord's plan for me when I go home? What is my future? It's always been, "Well, I go to high school and then go on a mission and on my mission I'll become an adult and know how to plan my life," but now, here I am, and I feel like a baby with no clue what to do when I go home.

Babies learn to walk step by step, so maybe that's what I'm supposed to do. I really believe that when the time comes to move on, I'll be able to handle it. I really don't know why I'm writing all this. Maybe I am a psycho and I should just do like they say and "don't worry, be happy." Live for today and find out what tomorrow brings when the time comes. Yeah, "eat, drink and be merry for tomorrow we die." The scriptures warn about that type of thinking and living. Do I believe that the scriptures are true? I keep thinking about them. Maybe I should just keep shoving it all out of my mind. Keep saying I know this is true even though I don't know what "true" is. It's all so clear if I don't think about it. If I just say ok, water ski in the summer, snow ski in the winter, fly fish, date chicks, and play hoop all year long. Those are the things that make me happy. Be cool, hang out, and just don't worry about it. Be good, do what these "scriptures" say. Go on a mission and teach people about eternity even though I don't comprehend it. Then, when judgment day comes I can say I did my duty.

Maybe that's what this "faith" is-just do what you're told, be the people the scriptures say are "true" and you'll get it all someday. I just wonder if it's too much to ask to know right now like the prophets. They saw God and God revealed unspeakable things to them. But how did they get their exceeding faith that allowed them to see and learn so much? Is it something that only certain people have and the rest of us just wait till we die? Well I've asked these questions till I'm just repeating myself. So now I'm going to do what I tell people every day to do-the same answer that I gave my Sunday school teachers since I could talk: read the scriptures and say my prayers, because if my answers aren't there I have no idea where to look. If it isn't in that or my faith is bu gou (not sufficient) then I guess I'll just keep going, following all these teachings because it's what I believe. In the end if they are not true at least I stuck to what I believe in.

But the sound that they're not true scares me so bad. That's a real feeling because I know that they are true. My logical sense says if they're not true I'm a nothing, life is nothing, I'm just not here. I always felt depressed when I heard the song that says, "all we are is dust in the wind." I won't accept that. To me God just has to be there. There has to be more than just this life. The question just is time. I think I wrote about time before-what is time? I'm too tired to get going on that one. I need some temporary sleep for a temporal P-day tomorrow when I can get some temporal happiness from some temporal basketball. At least that's within a time range I can grasp.

Hey! Maybe that's how Heavenly Father works-He gives us happiness within time chunks we can grasp. Like me, I'm dumb. I only grasp short time periods as long as I see a happy goal at the end of my time period. Maybe it's a hoop game, or a ski trip. Maybe it's a mission, then getting married, having babies, waiting for them to get old enough to do stuff with me, then waiting to retire, then the next cruise or a visit from children or whatever. Then death. All the short-term daily things that make life go fast keep it interesting, and make me get up in the morning so I can work toward that goal. Then, after I achieve it, look forward to the next. Well I'm back where I started. What about after? Do I shove that thought out and just live for P-day next week? Well, on goes life. I guess I'm just really finding out how limited mortal minds are. How do I expand it? PRAYER, READ THE SCRIPTURES, HAVE FAITH... well one thing is forever.

Can you see the circles in my thought process? Searching deeper and deeper into my religious beliefs to try to find a reason for the depression in my heart was a forming tornado spiraling and twisting in the clouds, working its way to earth with only a short time left before it touched down. The round and round effect reminds me of a silly song we used to sing while driving to Scout camp. Maybe you've heard it:

This is the song that never ends, yes it goes on and on my friend. Some people started singing it not knowing what it was, and they'll continue singing it forever just because this is the song that never ends, yes it goes on and on my friend. Some people started singing it not knowing what it was, and they'll continue singing it forever just because this is the song that never ends...

We would sing the song for what must have seemed like hours until our leaders finally would yell, "I'm going to go crazy if you don't stop singing that stupid song!" To which we would laugh and say,

Crazy? I went crazy once, they locked me in a room full of white rats. Rats? I hate rats. They'll drive you crazy! Crazy? I went crazy once. They locked me in a room full of white rats. Rats? I hate rats. They'll drive you crazy! Crazy...

Like these silly sayings, my thoughts constantly spun round and round, ever searching for a far-out, or deeply philosophic answer, and all the while not seeing the simple truth right before my eyes: I was mentally ill and needed help.

I think that most missionaries start asking themselves similar questions like the ones I did in my heartfelt journal entry. The beauty of a mission is the way it makes the missionaries themselves go through similar refining processes to decide whether or not the things they teach others are true. An extra stumbling block in my path, in addition to the normal potholes and speed bumps all missionaries encounter, was my perfectionist expectations mixed with a fear of ever admitting I needed help.

The journal entry says I didn't talk about my true feelings because people would think I was a freak. Rather than freak, a more accurate word would be imperfect. I feared if I admitted I had questions or problems, I wasn't an excellent or worthy missionary.

As a result, I developed some damaging habits. The first was always pretending to understand the Chinese I heard. In my mind, the worst thing I could say to someone was, "ting bu dong" (I don't understand). I feared if I said it, they would think I didn't have the Holy Spirit with me. It makes me sad to think of the learning and teaching opportunities I missed as a result of this stubbornness.

Another consequence of my "I have to be perfect or someone will find out I'm not" thinking was poor eating. Growing up, I never did enjoy or appreciate the art of cooking. When hunger hit in Tainan, the most creative work I could produce was a triple-decker PBJ sandwich. After moving, however, I couldn't find peanut butter or jelly where we shopped in Kaohsiung.

If I remember right, Kaohsiung was home to nine million people at that time, so breakfast and noodle shops were on every corner. American food, however, was as scarce as Americans. Rather than talk to my companion about my total lack of cooking ability and creativity, I tried to learn by secret observation.

At one of our dinner appointments we had what they called a huoguo. The direct translation is "fire pot." That's exactly what it was. They put a big pot filled with water on a hot burner. When the water boiled, they put different foods in. When the items were cooked everyone reached into the pot with their chopsticks, took pieces out, mixed them in a small bowl of rice, and then ate them. While watching for foods I liked and could use in my own cooking, I found most of the fire pot ingredients were foods I had never seen before. I felt too embarrassed to ask about them, so I never learned what they were called. All I recognized were shrimp and clams.

So, what did I buy when I went shopping for food? You guessed it-shrimp and clams. The only other things I recognized in the market we shopped at were canned corn and Snickers bars. So every

P-day I piled a week's worth in my basket, took them home, and stuffed them in the back of the old refrigerator. Then, whenever I was home for dinner, I enjoyed boiled shrimp and clams, cold corn-we didn't have a microwave to warm it with-and a nice Snickers bar to get it all down.

Another American missionary who we shared our apartment with offered to teach me a few dishes. However, like an ever-starving tapeworm, my pride chomped away any hint of imperfections inside me. All I could do was pretend that shrimp, clams, corn and Snickers were what I really wanted to eat-every day. I remember him shaking his head and saying, "You must really like corn."

I did have one other eating option. There was a noodle shop and arcade next door. That doesn't sound so bad, except I only knew how to order one thing and I wouldn't ask for help to read the menu. The owner of the tiny shop thought I loved that one dish, so he always had a huge grin on his face as he brought out my niu rou mian (beef noodles). The truth was that I could barely get it down! I don't know if the beef was bad or if the noodles were spoiled, but every time I ate there, I felt sick to my stomach for the next few hours.

So for two months, when we were home for dinner, I either ate shrimp, clams, corn, and Snickers, went hungry, or got semi-sick from the nasty noodles in the shop next door. Luckily, we were out on the town for most of our meals.

My new companion, Tacamora or, "Taco" as we called him, never seemed to notice my strange eating habits. He ate almost anything, including the shells, legs, heads and tails of my shrimp! We got along, though, and had many successes and wonderful experiences together.

Speaking of eating, receiving mail was like home cooking for missionaries. I knew if I wanted to feast on letters from home, I needed to send out a lot of mail. So every P-day, I got up extra early to write letters.

The payoff was great. Like a gravy train I received letters and packages almost every day. I started a ritual for opening my mail, arranging the letters in order of my interest. The ones from those I looked forward to hearing from the most I put at the bottom of the pile. Like dessert, I saved them for the last. The ones at the top of stack were usually mission business or letters from my parents.

I always opened Dawn's letters last, reading them slowly, and savoring every word. She wrote faithfully every week and often sent care packages. Her letters were full of nourishing encouragement, spicy news of school, sumptuous scriptures, and sweet spiritual thoughts. True to our agreement, she never wrote candy heart, lovie-dovie things.

The thing I looked forward to most was the way she closed her letters: sometimes with "love always," a quick, "I love you," or "yours always." Those few moments of reading her letters along with P-day mornings of writing letters to her, were all I allowed myself to think about her. Reading her letters assured me our relationship remained strong, and I found the ability to focus on the missionary work at hand most of the time.

After one month with Taco in Kaohsiung, I finally "finaled," meaning I passed off the memorization of all six missionary discussions in Mandarin. It took two months longer than I had planned and, as I started working on level two of the mission's language program, I felt as if I had been left behind. So, to catch up I started getting up a half hour earlier for extra language study time. I didn't realize my poor eating and lack of sleep were shortening my mental health fuse and an explosion was sizzling closer and closer.

Having my discussion memorization and the label of greenie behind me, time and responsibility seemed to pick up pace. When word of my next transfer arrived, I couldn't believe how quickly my time with Taco had raced to an end. The new transfer sent me up north to the county of Taichung, city of Wu Feng. Leaving Taco was difficult, but as the northbound train pushed onward, leaving behind the pollution and nasty noodles, I couldn't help but feel a clear forecast for refreshing change.

As we shook hands at the Taichung train station, my new companion introduced himself: Mike from Utah, with only two months left before he returned home to the USA. Mike then introduced a young Chinese man standing next to him. "This is Lin You Nan, but we just call him Yoner. He's an awesome church member in our area." After shaking hands, Yoner pointed at my suitcases and asked, "Can I help?"

"Sure," I replied gratefully. I was expecting to pack my luggage by bike to our new apartment. What delightful disappointment it was when Yoner led my companion and me to his car! Instead of a long bike ride in troubled traffic and humid heat, I enjoyed sitting in an automobile with cool air conditioning. It may not sound like much, but I hadn't been in a car since the initial van ride from the airport! What luxury! What ease! What comfort!

As Yoner drove I listened to him talk with my new companion. I could understand a word here and a word there, but not enough to follow the conversation. It was obvious they weren't talking about missionary work or spiritual things. It seemed that they were talking about business and the economy. Stopping at a red light, Yoner reached back his right arm and grabbed the headrest stretching his back and neck. Mike was just as comfortable-adjusting the air conditioning and even turning on the radio to a Chinese music station. These actions, though simple, left a lasting impression on me. These two were completely at ease together. There was no culture gap, no language barrier, no skin color, nose size, single or double eyelid-nothing. They were just two friends enjoying each other's company.

When their conversation dwindled, Yoner turned his head and started talking to me. He spoke in Chinese, but chose simple words that I understood. He asked about the missionary efforts in Kaohsiung, my former companion, and how I liked Taiwan so far. Before I knew it, I found myself relaxed, confidently speaking my limited Chinese to an interested and understanding ear. When I came to words that I hadn't learned in Chinese yet, I just threw in the English word and he seemed to understand perfectly. The hour drive flew by in what seemed like minutes. As Yoner helped carry my luggage into my new apartment, I felt sad he had to leave. "When will I see you again?" I asked.

"Don't worry," he laughed. "My work is right next door. We'll see each other all the time." For the next two months we did see each other often, almost every day. He gave us rides to church on Sundays. He accompanied us when we taught discussions. After long days of contacting many people and only obtaining a few referrals, we would come trudging into the car dealership where he worked. He encouraged us, made us laugh, and lifted our spirits.

Before I knew it, Mike went home and I was assigned a new companion, Aaron. Aaron was a legend among the missionaries because of his incredible Chinese language ability and cultural adaptation. If Chinese were music, Aaron had perfect pitch. From the minute our companionship started, we never spoke English to each other. Working in tune with Aaron, my language ability crescendoed, and after one short month together, I passed off my second level and started on the third and last level of language acquisition.

Aaron enjoyed Yoner's friendship as much as I did, so we continued seeing him almost daily. Our time together, however, was quickly coming to a close because Yoner had also decided to serve a mission. His mission assignment sent him to the north Taiwan mission in Taipei. As the time for him to leave drew near, Yoner and I had many personal conversations. He told me how he was the only Christian in his family. His parents, especially his father, thought it was a foolish waste of time and money for him to quit his job and serve a mission.

Yoner told me how he loved and respected his parents and how he wanted to make them proud of him. He told me how in most Chinese families, the parents, especially the father, rarely if ever tells his children he loves them. Yoner wanted to tell his father he loved him, but couldn't. I doubt he had ever said wo ai ni (I love you) to anyone. He said the best way for him to show his love was to be an example of righteousness and to go on his mission-even though his parents didn't understand why.

I remember the rainy night before Yoner left for Taipei. Aaron and I arrived home at the same time as darkness. Wanting to get in out of the rain, Aaron quickly locked up his bike and sprinted toward our apartment. It took me a little longer to lock up my bike. Just as I turned to follow Aaron, Yoner pulled next to me up in his car. I remember huddling under my umbrella while leaning on his window talking to him. He was nervous about leaving on his mission the next day and needed encouragement. I told him how bang (awesome) he would be and how I knew that he would touch the lives of many people.

After the brief but meaningful conversation, Yoner looked at me and said, "Hao An Di, wo ai ni (Andy Hogan, I love you)." He reached up from his car window and got soaking wet from the rain as we hugged. I asked him if he had anyone to write to him. He said, "probably not." I told him I would write to him every week.

Every P-day for the next few weeks, I wrote Yoner faithfully. Writing letters in Chinese helped improve my language quite a bit; however, it took me an hour or two just to write a few simple sentences. Yoner must have sensed my dilemma because one week, instead of a letter, I received a small package with a voice tape inside. How thrilling it was to hear his voice and to have 60 minutes with him. From that point, I threw out the letter writing and began carrying a little, black, portable tape recorder everywhere I went. Through the treasured tapes we shared many missionary experiences.

One time, while making a tape for Yoner, sharing with him the challenges some of the people we were teaching had, I told him how much I had prayed for them and how much desire I had for them to obtain happiness. Right in the middle of the sentence I stopped. I clicked off the tape and thought to myself, "I really care for these people I'm working with–and for Yoner. I have become a part of their marvelous culture and I really feel love for them!"

The sweet realization of this miraculous change moved me to tears and, clicking on my tape recorder, I told Yoner how grateful I was for his open-hearted friendship. I said I knew God had sent me to Wu Feng to meet Yoner so he could open the door of fellowship into the Chinese culture and let me in.

In his return tape, Yoner told me how grateful he was to know me and how he knew Heavenly Father had brought us together for his benefit as well. He said before he knew me, he had never verbally expressed his love. After coming to know me, however, he had found the ability to do so. Yoner told me about a Chinese expression called yuan fen. He said it's an unexplainable feeling that you knew someone before this life and, when you meet for the first time, you feel like old friends. "Yuan fen," he said, "is the good luck or pre-destiny that brings those friends together." He said our relationship had beautiful yuan fen.

I believe my friendship with Yoner made my time in Wu Feng pass without heavy symptoms of depression. Besides family, a true and loving friend is the greatest source of comfort and peace that a person suffering from mental illness can have. In just a couple of short, wonderful months, Yoner became more than a friend; he became a big brother.

The same time Yoner left for Taipei, Aaron also was transferred. My new companion was Brent from American Fork, Utah. For the most part we got along well and had great success together. One month later, I received a surprise notice that I was being transferred to a city, way in the south, called Chao Chou and become a senior companion (the more experienced of the two missionaries serving together).

Moving away from Wu Feng stung harder than leaving my previous two areas because I had come to truly love the people in that town. Still, becoming senior companion and being a leader was what I had worked like a busy bee for. Now, I accepted Chao Chou as my honey-sweet opportunity to really make a buzz. I had no idea the kind of hornet's nest I was about to drop on the mission.

Chapter 7
Chao Chou

At first, moving to Chao Chou seemed extra special for several reasons. First, the small town was so far south that the scenery changed from concrete, crowds, and coughing cars, to trees, clean air, non-polluted beaches, and even fish in the streams. With many small towns, there were a lot of "fishing holes" for fishers of men to choose from. The closest missionaries were an hour's train ride north in the city of Ping Tung or a two-hour bus ride to the city of Hung Chun to the south. Everything in between was my area. The other reason for liking the move waited to greet me at the train station. He was a native Taiwanese companion, Buo Sen.

When my train came to a stop at the one-bench station, he greeted me with a genuine smile. We threw my luggage on our bikes and rode to a little lunch stop that had to be the dirtiest dive I had ever seen. It looked like a three-sided lean-to built with rusty nails, scrap wood, and a spoiled lime-green tarp draped over the top. Hanging from the ceiling, an oscillating fan stirred up the hot air. Sticky black gunk, that looked like spider web in an exhaust pipe, caked so thickly on the cage of the fan that pieces occasionally blew off and splattered on the walls, floor, and eating tables. Watching a rat sneak around in the shadows,

I nervously ordered some fried rice and then covered it up with my hands as I ate to keep the fan gunk from falling in.

While we ate, Buo Sen told me about the missionary work in the area. Hearing the many challenges my new area faced, I was amazed at his positive attitude and happy tone. While each of my other three areas had all blossomed like a peach tree in springtime to over one hundred active and contributing church members-enough to build a church house–Chao Chou was still feeling the freeze and barely budding with just five church members who came regularly. Instead of a big beautiful chapel, Chao Chou's meetinghouse was just a rented apartment next to an arcade.

Like the building structure, the leadership of the church in Chao Chou was also fragile. Buo Sen laughed as he told me how the missionaries had to call the local Chao Chou leader on the phone each week and ask if he planned on attending the meetings on Sunday. Never mind getting him to fulfill his responsibilities, just coaxing him into coming was a major task. Instead of the local leader, it was the missionaries who carried the burden of preparing and presenting sermons and lessons each Sunday. The missionaries also administered the sacrament, handled the offerings, paid the bills, and basically did everything the local leader was supposed to do.

When Buo Sen asked if I knew how to lead music, I told him, "Yes, and I know how to play a few hymns on the piano."

Hearing this, he clapped his hands with joy. "Now we won't have to sing a cappella all the time," he rejoiced.

I took it as a great compliment that the mission president, President Watson, trusted me enough to send me to this, "the toughest area in the mission" as he later called it. Buo Sen's optimism and enthusiasm also excited me. As we rode our bikes home and I listened to him yell "wang wang wang" at a dog that started chasing him (You didn't expect Chinese dogs to bark in English did you?) I couldn't wait to get started on a long and fun companionship with him. It turned out that our companionship only lasted for one month.

Voice Tape to Lin You Nan (Yoner) From Chao Chou
Dear Yoner, thanks for sending your last voice tape. It's great to hear you are doing well in your first area and that you get along with your companion. You and I are both getting pretty good at talking into these tape machines while we ride our bikes through crazy Taiwan traffic. I think the

traffic in your city is much worse than here though. This southern country town, Chao Chou, is tiny; quite a contrast from the crowded and polluted cities I've already served in. Here I love seeing the green hills, banana forests and even fish in the streams! It's a beautiful area to work in.

As far as the missionary work here, things are going okay. I was with Buo Sen for only a month when we went down to Hung Chun for a meeting and there received word that he was moving. To be honest, the news shocked me, and I told another missionary, "Wo wan dan le. (I'm dead.)" Buo Sen and I had become such good friends and he knew this place so well. Now, I'm on my own and I don't know if I can handle all the responsibility. It was very hard to see him leave.

My new companion is a young man from Oregon named Sonny. He has been on island for four and a half months. So technically he's not a greenie. But he might as well be. First, he really struggles with the language. The other day he tried to ask a seven-year-old child, "Ni yao qu nali? (Where are you going?)" The little boy looked up at him and said, "Ting bu dong. (I don't understand.)" It broke my heart to hear the child say that to him, and so I set a goal to do everything I could to help Sonny learn the language quickly.

Last week we memorized the whole fourth discussion together! I remember how when I was a junior companion, my senior companions never helped me, and it took three whole months to pass them all off. With Sonny as my junior, I set a goal to help him final in one month. We've worked on it pretty hard. First we translated it into English. Next I taught it to him in Chinese, then I helped him memorize it. After working together, he passed off a whole discussion in one week! Before, it took him four months to memorize the first three. People sure can do a lot with a little encouragement.

Yesterday we had a discussion with a young high school student. He has been studying religion for a long time. I told him, "We've already taught you much truth. Once you hear truth you have to choose if you will follow it or not." I said, "You will be held accountable for what you know." It really hit him hard, and he committed to read the scriptures and really think and pray about the truth we have taught him. I hope he gets an answer.

Well, big bro, it looks like I'm about out of time. I can't wait to hear how things are going up north. Jia you! Jia you! (Go, go, go!) And remember, wo ai ni. (I love you.)

Remember in an earlier chapter I pointed out that one of my early symptoms of mania was obsessive thinking? Or, in other words, getting hung up on something with no way of getting it out of my head? Before I came to Chao Chou, the thoughts usually left with a good night's sleep. But by this time, the obsession with truth stayed with me from the time I stumbled out of bed in the morning until I fell onto the covers at night. You can see in the recording I sent to Yoner how I spread my grandiose plans and perfectionist expectations, other symptoms of mania, around me like the stench of our unwashed dishes piled up in the kitchen crying silently for attention. Now, not only did I expect impossible excellence of myself, but also I started demanding it of the people I taught, and especially my companion.

While researching for this book, I contacted Sonny and asked him to share his memories. He recalls,

You became consumed with proving truth. You tried to relate everything to it. From the scriptures we read in companionship study to the things people would say in response to your questions, you always had to "prove truth." You started getting weird and consumed with these things. This behavior put me in a real tough situation. The situation was that you were thought of very highly by other missionaries and the mission president. I didn't feel like I could talk to anyone about what was going on with your bizarre behavior. There weren't any other missionaries in our area either. It was just me and you. Still, I never could have dreamed what was about to happen. I had no experience to prepare me for things getting so out of control. Your behavior changed so slowly it almost seemed normal for you until the last day.

Poor Sonny had to live with me and suffer the brunt of my swelling mania day after day. In the tape to Yoner, I made it sound as if I was the loving, caring senior companion who could give Sonny perfect language use, perfect teaching skills, and perfect discussion memorization and mastery. After all, I helped him pass off his fourth discussion in one week!

What really happened was after a week of intense grueling, I deemed him ready to pass off his discussion. Ignoring his pleas of, "I don't feel ready," I set up the appointment. The next day we rode the train to Ping Tung where Michael Hinds, our mission leader for the county of Ping Tung, was stationed. Outside the classroom where Sonny and Michael were meeting, I paced the floor like a guard on maximum-security duty. When they finished, the door opened and Sonny trudged out looking like a cat that had been thrown into a rice paddy irrigation ditch. Behind Sonny, Michael walked out, quietly pulled me aside and whispered, "I passed him off, but next time he needs to be given more preparation time."

The only part of the sentence I heard was, "I passed him off," which convinced me I was right in the way I had "helped" him.

This same "help" attacked Sonny following a difficult visit with a man named Zheng, who had been a strong church member at one time but had fallen into complete inactivity. Zheng told us he believed in God, but he just got bored with the church and would come back only when it had something more to offer him. After the appointment, while we were discussing how we could help Zheng come back, Sonny kidded, "Someone just needs to smack him upside the head with a brick."

I didn't laugh. I didn't smile. For a moment all I could do was glare. "If Sonny knew about true Christ-like love, he would never say something like that," I thought to myself. "The whole reason Zheng fell away was that he didn't feel love. Now, here we are, the one contact he still has with the church, the one contact who can love him enough to bring him back, but all we can say is, 'Let's do it with violence; hurt him even more than he already is by smacking him upside the head with a brick.'"

From that time on, just about everything Sonny did bugged me, but I kept my criticism inside and let stinging irritation grow. I knew what I should be like, but I couldn't figure out why my thoughts and feelings wouldn't allow it. My journal entries from that time are full of thoughts like, "I should encourage him instead of criticize him. I should lift him up instead of knock him down. I should love him instead of despise him."

The shower of shoulds washed me under a pile of pressure and splashed up an even lengthier list of goliath goals. The more irritated and aggravated the mania caused me to be, the more I expected of myself and the harder I pushed myself. Remember the card I kept in my scriptures? By this time the list of expectations I had for myself, to be completed before the end of my mission, had filled that card on both sides. The codes were as follows:

Bible: Read the entire Bible in Chinese.
C&EMS: Have my calling and election made sure.

LAPAet: Learn to always have a positive attitude to influence and motivate those around me-enthusiasm.

Decide: Decide my major and plan my school goals for the next five years-decide what to do for a career.

DBP: Dunk Before Plane-slam-dunk a standard basketball on a standard court before the plane ride home.

Journal: Write in my journal at least every P-day.

Doll: Find and buy the special China doll that Mother asked for.

Ke: Review from memory at least a principle a day from the missionary discussions.

Leech Book: Make a dictionary from all my leech books to leave for new missionaries. (A leech book was a small spiral notebook that I carried in my pocket. When I heard words that I didn't understand, I wrote them down and then looked them up when I got home. I had four or five filled notebooks of words I had leeched by that point in my mission.)

Pray: Learn to use the power of prayer as a means of questions and answers-praying to someone and feeling it.

50 a day: Memorize 50 new Chinese characters every day.

Taigee: Learn to teach the discussions in Taiwanese.

It makes me tired just writing all of them down again. By the way, I did buy the China doll and sent it home to Mother. These goals were secret. No one knew of them or the sense of inner guilt that grew each day as I failed to live up to them. The missionaries I reported to, and the mission president who reviewed their reports, all saw a hard-working missionary, powering the work in Chao Chou forward like a locomotive pulling a heavy load over the mountain.

"You're doing great," President Watson encouraged in an interview. "Keep up the good work." President Watson had no idea I had a mental illness and was heading for a derailment. Following my first breakdown, some people blamed him for putting me in such a difficult area. I don't blame President Watson. Working in an area like Chao Chou was what I wanted most. I worked hard to be the best, and everyone, except Sonny, saw the shining outward efforts and image. I was the only one who knew I wasn't as strong as I seemed.

To keep my image and production up to the grandiose standards I felt they had to be, my sleeping and eating habits took a terrible turn for the worse. I stayed up later and later, making phone calls to read scriptures with the people we had contacted and were teaching, talk to them about their concerns, or to set up appointments. The mission rules said "lights out by 10:30." At 10:30 we turned out the lights so Sonny could sleep while I continued to talk on the phone, thinking the deep conversations were more important than going to bed. I also forced myself to wake up earlier and earlier in order to make more time for study. The missionary rules also stated that we should "arise at 6:30." I started getting up at 5:00 or earlier.

Like the mice that hid behind our pantry, my despicable diet also chomped away at my mental health. The only place I knew to get food was the filthy dive next to the train station where Buo Sen and I had always eaten. After eating there a few times, Sonny refused to go back.

"Where do you want to go then?" I asked.

"You choose," he said with a sincere smile.

Rather than take heart at his offer of kindness, his reply infuriated me. In my mind, a senior companion should know all the good eating-places in his area. He should be able to read the signs in front of the restaurants. And he should surely know how to order a whole mess of meals. I could do none of these. With shame and embarrassment on the inside and rage on the outside, I rode to the closest shop, threw my bike down, and stormed in.

When I asked if they had egg fried rice, niu rou mian, or niu pai, the only dishes I knew how to say, they replied that they didn't sell them. I could only read one other dish on the menu, "bai fan," so I ordered it for both of us.

With my brain steaming and Sonny looking at me as if I was psycho (almost, but not yet), we sat down to dinner with two bowls of white rice-and nothing else. After we had eaten for a minute, the owner, with a pitying look in his eye, quietly walked over carrying a pan. Without a word, he scooped up some broth and poured it onto our rice. I don't remember if I had the courtesy to say xie xie (thanks), but I remember how good the rice tasted with some sauce on it.

Most of the time, we ate at our apartment. Chao Chou was so far south there were no American stores of any kind. The one tiny supermarket in town sold only Taiwanese and Japanese food.

My weekly grocery list consisted of the following: frozen shrimp, clams, and shwei jiao (a type of dumpling), Taiwanese pudding, pao mian (Taiwanese equivalent of Ramen noodles), canned corn, and powdered milk. I didn't even know how to use an electric rice cooker to fix white rice! Rather than study lessons on food and cooking, or ask the members or friends to teach me, I started despising eating and didn't even want to talk about it. I started skipping meals in order to study and do "important things." I believe my poor and irregular diet contributed to my first breakdown as much as my perfectionism, poor sleeping, grandiose goals, the pressure of the struggling congregation, and everything else.

The funny thing about extreme mania is, at first it feels great. I mean incredibly wonderful. Answers to prayers seemed to descend like alpine snows while flakes of inspiration and revelation piled like powder in the aspens. One night while praying, I thought direct revelation started coming to me. In the dark I opened my journal and wrote down what I thought were specific instructions for a discussion we were scheduled to teach the next day. What I should say and how the person would react were all included in the "revelation."

Part of being a missionary means believing in personal revelation. The question then becomes, how can a young, 20 year old missionary know the difference between a long distance, direct phone call from God, and simple heartburn stemming from too much MSG on the missionary's pao mian (Chinese equivalent to Ramon noodles)? Here are my thoughts: What I received that night couldn't have been revelation for a couple of reasons. First of all, the things I wrote in my journal never happened. The day after the "revelation," my mind was so flighty I didn't even remember what I wrote.

Secondly, my companion didn't receive any "revelations" or even feel peace around me. I believe God puts us on earth with other people so we can give each other feedback and help each other along the way. If there was a real revelation to be received at that time, I'm sure it would have come through Sonny. He could have (and probably would have jumped at any invitation) told me I was overboard and "going off the deep-end." The reality I couldn't see was that while Sonny floated safely above me in the boat of reality while I was drowning in deep, manic water.

The ability to humbly listen to my companion's view could have warned me that not only was I sinking, but a terrible monster was also swimming closer and closer. At that point I still had my head above water and had the ability to reason and to listen. In other words, it was still my choice to talk honestly with someone and ask for help.

I didn't listen. I didn't ask for help. With my confusion between spirituality and reality, I guess a complete breakdown was the only way God could open my eyes to the illness that was creeping up and getting set to drag me under. I hope and pray that others reading my story can learn from my experience and not have to fall so low in order to ask for help, or to honestly face inner struggles.

As I unknowingly sank closer and closer to the breaking point, a tsunami of outward emotional bliss started rolling, bowling over the irritability and guilt, and barreling in a runaway rage of glee that felt even better than kissing Dawn at Wampus, or being captain of the winning team in the high school state championship track and field meet. I started waking up feeling as if I had never slept, but energized and motivated.

Oddly enough, we started experiencing success in our missionary work like never before. We spent my last couple of Saturdays in the small, apartment church house doing nothing but teaching all day. I remember the attendance in our Sunday church meetings consistently surpassed 20, whereas before, we were lucky to get ten. One Monday, at the home of a family we were working with, 26 people showed up to hear the missionary lessons! It was amazing how good everything seemed to be going.

Interested people started popping out of the cracks and alleys to find us. I remember one night while riding our bikes home, a small group of young college students pulled up next to us on bullet bikes and called out, "We want to talk to you about Jesus!" We set up an appointment with them. They came and were sincerely interested. Sonny and my statistical reports at the end of each week far excelled the average of the mission.

All the success fed the fire of my deep thinking and obsession with truth. After a few weeks with my fuse burning at both ends, the time had come for something to blow. I remember my last night in our apartment, talking on the phone with a "golden" member. His name was Zhong. We called him "golden" because in two weeks, he had read the entire Bible (That makes the goal on my secret card sound like cake, doesn't it?), listened to all six missionary discussions, and received baptism. Through the process Zhong called me every night to discuss his favorite scriptures. After we baptized him, the phone calls continued.

This night, we again talked about his favorite scriptures and how they applied to his life. Then we talked about life in general. The conversation turned personal-like friends supporting each other rather than a teacher and a student.

I really opened up to him. As I did, I found myself talking about feelings I had never looked in the face before. I told him about the secret, tumultuous mental battles I was having and how "youshihou, wo pa wo zhende yao fa feng (sometimes I fear that I really might go crazy)." I said it in all sincerity, as I wiped tears from my eyes. He soothed and comforted me, saying he would come help us do our missionary work the next day.

Chapter 8
The First Breakdown

When I got out of bed at 5:00 in the morning, I didn't know if I had slept or not. Because it was P-day, I got out my journal and started writing. As you read, keep in mind this was the climax of a mental explosion. In other words, don't try too hard to understand and make sense of it all. I don't share this to try to teach any manner of doctrine. Some aspects may be true; perhaps much is false. However, what is or is not true isn't the point. The reason I share this journal entry is to reveal my circling thought processes and to make some sense of the nonsense that followed.

Journal entry 1991-10-28, P-day, Chao Chou
As I look back on this week, I realize that the Lord has really taught me quite a bit. I think I've learned what I'm looking for. First, what is truth? If I don't understand what it is, how can I teach it? In order to have truth you have to have a true background; something that, no matter time or circumstance, will still remain the same. If it changes then it isn't true. It doesn't matter if it is teachings, guidance or direction, the same applies. It has to come from a perfect source. God is the source that we claim. If He is true, He will remain true. It doesn't matter if people believe in Him or not. God is the source of truth forever and ever. So this week as I realized that I

believe in this God, I've started to try to rely on this truth and I've found myself happy and successful in His work.

One of the other things I've learned is the Lord's method of solving problems through the proper leaders. I see the problems here in Chao Chou, and it seems to be that because the leaders haven't been used as they should to solve problems, the small congregation has suffered.

It's so important to go to the proper leader so he can use his authority to solve problems permanently. If I don't use the proper leader then, first, I'm stealing the responsibility of the leader who has authority of God and I don't; and second, the thing usually won't be fixed permanently because I'm not entitled to revelation for that thing. If I use the proper leaders, then I don't have to deal with too many problems. In other words, the promise of the Lord comes true that I won't have more than I can handle because the leaders do what they are supposed to, making my load light and easy.

So, who is my leader and where can he help? That's what I need to ask myself each time I have a problem. If I do this, I know the problem will get fixed as it should. I don't have to solve all the problems myself. I just have to help my leaders to do what they should, then do what they say and follow the counsel they give.

I am realizing that the best way to show our trust and faith in the Lord is by using the leaders he has given us. If we try to solve problems alone, then it shows we don't trust him; it shows that we think that we are smarter than Him and that we don't need or want His help. If everyone would do their part in solving problems the church would flourish and everyone would be able to handle their heavy loads.

But, the first step is for us to fix ourselves; realize where we need to go to fix problems, then use the power of discernment that God has given us to know what is right or wrong. If we find that it is wrong, then we need to go to the right leader to fix it or we have the same problem and need to fix ourselves first-pull the beam from our own eye-I think that's what the scripture meant there. I just realized how that comes in with following rules. If I have a rule that is given and I have a problem with and disobey it, then I ...

Scribble, scribble, scribble...

This is what I found: my mortal mind stops right here. That right there is the answer that I've been searching for, and when I understand it, I will have found the answer to the questions that I've longed for for so long. Is God, God? Yes! Then there is no problem. That's what that equation says. Everything turns to God no matter what, when I...

I just lost it, but I found it again, now I know why, because I believe in God, I know He lives, I know He loves us. I know that if I lose this knowledge that I've gained then it's me that is lost and not God, because God lives. I now know why. Why? Because God lives. That's it. That's all there is.

As the Chinese say, "waasay!" As a Utah surfer says, "Whoa dude, that's some pretty heavy brine shrimp!" I know what you're thinking: "So what was the scribble, scribble, scribble part? What was the thing that you found that you lost, then found again, but never wrote? What was it? Tell me! Tell me! Tell me!"

What I discovered, dear friends, was the secret of eternity and divinity! It was the answer of all problems in the universe! I write it in full sarcasm now, but at that time, it is what I believed I had just proven. It was the result of several hours staring at my journal, thinking–obsessing–about problems, solutions and trying to figure out the root cause of my misery-without admitting anything was wrong with me. Before I scribbled it out, fearing that if I wrote it or said it I would be destroyed, I had written:

God

Man   Love

This was the secret truth triangle. I was convinced when a person understood it, he discovered God! The reasoning was this: every problem of man could be answered with God and proven with love. In other words, no matter what problem man had, his ultimate answer was always "God," and the proper authority to learn of God was love.

The whole secret of the truth triangle was that if you knew it you became a part of the solution (God, who included happiness, success, healing, understanding and everything else good that can solve people's problems). By saying the solution, instead of letting the person go through the proper authority to find it (love), you suddenly lost your true source and became the problem (man, who included everything weak, failing, sick, depressed, etc.) again. [Did I explain it lovingly?] Feeling as high as heaven, and thinking I had literally become a part of "God," I ran and found Sonny and tried to explain the truth triangle to him.

Have you ever played "guess what I'm thinking"? You give clues, but others must figure it out themselves. Poor Sonny. I'm sure I told him that I loved him a dozen times, but he still didn't admit he had a problem or ask about God. I explained it over and over-always careful to step around the truth (that I was, and he could be, a part of God). Finishing my explanation for the last time, I told him I loved him and asked, "Do you know what this means?"

"It means that I don't know what you're talking about," Sonny said, shaking his head and walking away.

"Then you need to find truth," I snapped back in the most loving tone I could.

With that, our free time for P-day ended, we hopped on our bikes, rode to the post office to send out some letters and then pedaled toward the church. As promised, golden Zhong was waiting to meet us there. When I saw him, I dropped my bike and ran over to him yelling, "Wo zhao dao zhenli! Wo zhao dao zhenli! (I found truth! I found truth!)" Sharing my enthusiasm, Zhong listened intently as I explained the truth triangle. He didn't get it at first, but after a long explanation and a lot of coaching, I asked, "So how do you know when the person finds God?"

"He uses love to teach it," Zhong replied.

"Wo ai ni. (I love you.)" I said, winking at him.

He looked at me for a minute, then with hesitation replied, "Wo ye ai ni. (I love you too.)"

Let me explain the significance of his reply. Remember in a previous chapter where I wrote about my buddy Yoner? In that chapter I explained that Yoner had probably never told anyone that he loved them. This is typical. Traditional Chinese are a very reserved people. Verbally expressing love is not something they do freely. It isn't that they don't feel love. The Chinese are an extremely loving people. However, they show their love with actions rather than say it with words.

Talking Zhong into saying those three words put him in a very awkward place. I would be surprised if he had ever said them to anyone before. Knowing how personal it was for him to say that, and convinced he understood that he was now a part of "God," I threw my arms up in triumph and yelled, "That proves that we were friends before this life and will be friends forever!" I jumped over and gave him a great big hug.

Public displays of affection are as rare in the traditional Chinese culture as personal proclamations of love. I'm sure by this time he sensed something was very wrong.

While we were talking and hugging, a heavy rain started falling. When I got on my bike to ride to our appointment, Sonny noticed my book bag was missing. We looked around for a minute but couldn't find it. Sonny said we should skip our appointment and keep looking for it. I looked at my watch. "We have a ten minute bike ride to Sister Dai's house and we are already five minutes late. If God wants us to have the bag, it will turn up," I said. "Let's go."

"But the bag has all our contacts and appointments in it!" Sonny protested. Ignoring him, I got on my bike and started riding toward our appointment. I didn't even care that I had left my umbrella back at the apartment. I felt higher than the rain clouds and brighter than the veiled sun. "I love you!" I yelled, waving at the cars that splashed past, "Wo zhende ai ni! (I truly love you!)"

All this time, Zhong hadn't said much. As I plowed down the road, he held back and rode along next to Sonny. Arriving at the small apartment complex, I dropped my bike and walked to the doorway-dripping wet.

Sister Dai was a baptized member of the church but never came to church meetings or activities. Her husband rarely came home to see her or their children. In fact, we had never seen him. Besides caring for a new baby, alone, Sister Dai also had other children. The oldest was a son who must have been ten or eleven. During every previous visit, this young boy had screamed, fussed, whined, and teased so much that we never found the ability to carry on a simple spiritual conversation with her.

When Zhong and Sonny arrived, I gathered them together outside the apartment door. "The reason we can't bring God to Sister Dai is because the son doesn't feel love." I coached, "This time, I'll give the young boy love and you guys teach Sister Dai truth."

We rang the bird-whistling doorbell and heard a fluttering sound of footsteps immediately coming to answer. The door opened a crack. The young boy peered out. I kneeled down to his level and said, "Di di, ni hao. (Hello little brother.)" He spit in my face, then slammed the door and ran away laughing. A few seconds later, the door opened again. Sister Dai, holding the baby and looking like she hadn't slept in a week, opened the door with a forced smile. She hesitantly invited us in.

Seeing I was soaking wet, she kindly offered me a towel. I dabbed the towel on my face, not even thinking about how wet I was. We sat down, but before we were able to begin a conversation, the boy started throwing pens and pencils at us. As his mother started to stand to discipline him, I jumped up. "Rang wo lai (I'll do it)," I said, smiling.

77

Usually she would be embarrassed by this, but she was so tired she slumped back in her chair without saying anything. When the boy saw me coming, he dashed into the other room. With a quick glance at Sonny and Zhong, I winked, nodded my head, and followed the boy into the room.

The room looked and smelled like an indoor landfill. Ripped magazines, boxes, broken appliances, toys, and all kinds of other junk was piled up halfway to the ceiling. As I scanned the room, I spotted the boy hiding under a small table. Seeing the table was against the wall, with boxes of magazines and books blocking the sides, I quickly and quietly sat down in front of his only exit. "Do you want to hear a story?" I asked.

"Bu yao! (No!)" the boy blasted back.

"Hao jiu, hao jiu yiqian... (A long time ago...)" I began. I proceeded to tell him the story of Jesus appearing to his people after He had been resurrected. "Jesus called the children to come to Him and then He blessed them and loved them," I continued. As I told the story, I reached out my hand and felt a small hand timidly take it. I pulled him onto my lap and put my arms around him. He was silent and still as I told him that Jesus loved him just as He loved the little children in the story.

From that point on, a little angel replaced the little devil. We talked and played games with his toys. Every now and then when he reverted to being naughty to get attention, I "took my love away" by paying attention to something else. When he behaved, I gave him complete and undivided attention and affection. The boy responded exactly as I wanted him to. I felt I had complete control.

While we played, I glanced out the door to see Sonny and Zhong talking quietly with Sister Dai. In her arms, the baby was sleeping. Sister Dai had a smile on her face. "It's true. It's really, really true!" I thought to myself.

An hour later, as we said goodbye, the little boy clung to me while Sister Dai thanked us over and over for coming. I knelt down, gave the little boy a hug and said, "Remember God loves you." The boy still didn't want me to go, but the mother pulled him away and we quickly left.

With the rain stopped and the sun now sinking out of site, we started pedaling toward our apartment. Sonny rode way ahead. I saw him stop near a field next to a child he found hiding under a bush. I rode over to see a little girl huddled in a ball, crying. Shoving Sonny out of the way, I asked the girl, "Shemma shi? (What's wrong?)" She said something back in Taiwanese.

Zhong said, "Her mom and dad are fighting."

I don't remember the complete conversation with the child, but I remember telling her God loved her and He sent us to help her. It took a little coaxing, but I finally talked her into taking us to her house. She sat on the rack on the back of my bike, directing us to a tiny house that looked more like the scrap-lumber shack back at my parent's home in Utah where they stored the lawn mower.

Outside, a lady swept the dirt walkway. When she saw us she said, "W-w-wo ye sh-sh-shi JiDu tu." (I-I-I am a-a-also a Christian.)" Hearing the stammering in her speech, I thought she was mentally challenged. Looking back now, perhaps the funny breathing and the stammered speech could have reflected recently completed sobbing.

We knocked on the slivery, unpainted wooden door. A gruff-looking man answered. Seeing we had his daughter with us, he motioned for us to come into the one room shack. We followed him in. Without a word, he sat down at a table and started eating. "We found your daughter in a field, crying under a bush," I said. He nodded but didn't say anything. "If you're interested in knowing how to find love, ask your daughter where we came from."

With that, I motioned for Sonny and Zhong to leave. Ignoring me, Sonny pulled a Bible from his bag and offered it to the man. "He doesn't need that." I snapped in English so the man wouldn't understand. "He now has truth, and if he wants God, his desire for love will bring him to us. Come on."

Sonny ignored me again and tried to tell the man that we were Christian missionaries and let him know the location of our church house. I grabbed Sonny by the arm and pulled him outside. Steaming mad, he got on his bike and pedaled away. Zhong and I followed him. He rode to the church.

"Why did you come here?" I screamed. "Is it because you need the answers that this church offers?"

"I'm sick of this truth thing!" Sonny yelled back.

"Of course you are. You're still just a man!" I snarled.

With that, Sonny stomped into the church. I stood there thinking, "If he is in the church, then he is where he can find truth. That means my duties are done—and I am free!"

In manic glee I ran next door to the arcade and looked at the different video games. "Now I'm free, I can do whatever I want! I can even play video games!" I thought.

"Ni hao (Hello)", came a voice.

I looked over and saw a man sitting behind a desk at the end of the store. "I heard some shouting next door. Is everything okay?" he asked.

"Oh, that was just me and my companion fighting," I said, pulling a chair over to where he sat. "He's having a hard time finding truth."

"You know, sometimes I wonder that same question," the man said.

"This is my next duty as God!" I thought. "This man wants truth!" I then proceeded to talk to him about finding love.

At this point, the manic attack rose from severe to extreme. My memories from then on are only flashes—much like remembering a dream. It was the end of a floating high-above-the-clouds dream and the beginning of a horrific, real-life nightmare. Once I asked my psychiatrist what exactly happens during extreme mania. He replied that the brain goes through a literal chemical change that completely distorts thinking and reality perception. In other words the more the chemicals change, the less control the person has.

After using the church phone to call for help from our closest missionary leader, Michael in Ping Tung, Sonny found me at the arcade telling the man I was God. Sonny picked me up by the armpits and dragged me back to the church. By this time, I had lost most of my thought control. However, I still could sense that something was terribly wrong. Sadly, I didn't realize it was my mind that was sick. Instead, I thought I had entered a spiritual world where everything I heard, thought, said and did had eternal consequences. I perceived things as simple as swallowing, the sound of a motor-scooter outside, needing to use the restroom, or even the dripping of a rain gutter as messages and tests that I had to pass to get to God. My mind told me if I failed the tests, my soul would be damned.

Not knowing what else to do and terrified of making a wrong choice, I fell to my knees and prayed and prayed. My mind felt like a black, spinning abyss and I was falling into it deeper and deeper. I begged God to make it all a dream and to let me wake up. Oh, how I wanted to just wake up! I didn't wake up. Unable to bear more tests, still on my knees on the church floor, I huddled in a ball, clenched my eyes shut and refused to open them for hours. I started praying out loud, sometimes screaming, to drown out all other noises and invasive thoughts.

During this time, my county mission leader, Michael, caught a taxi and came to the church in Chao Chou. A little while later, the other missionary leader from the next closest county, Aaron, also came. They sat down next to me as I continued to kneel on the floor praying. They spoke with me and tried to comfort and pacify me while President Watson made the long drive down from Taichung to Chao Chou.

I didn't pray the whole time. At one point, I thought Michael was Jesus. I hugged him affectionately for several minutes. Suddenly, something jolted my thinking and told me that Michael had deceived me. Thinking he was the devil, I tried over and over to "cast him away". Michael and Aaron put up with this and much, much more. The details described in their journals and in my broken memories are almost too much to bear. I'm sure it was the longest 4 or 5 hours of their lives.

President Watson later described his memory of the experience:
I arrived in Chao Chou very late at night. You were at the chapel. When I got there, you were on the floor in an exhausted, yet still delusional state. You had tussled with Michael and even bit him. I remember the bite on his leg was an ugly, large, purple, mouth-shaped bruise that was bleeding. As I recall, you had been restrained many times perhaps by your companion and two other missionaries. You looked like you had been in a fight...completely disheveled, sweat soaked, rumpled, flushed, and out of gas. It was shocking and frightening.

We took you in the car to a hospital. You sat in the back seat between two missionaries who were to help restrain you in the event of struggle. As I recall, you were rather exhausted and passive but still not thinking clearly. You were subdued and exhausted. Almost like a blank stare. Your cognitive skills were impaired and you had to be soothed by having the missionaries or me talk to you and try to comfort you.

The hospital we went to was somewhere near Kaohsiung. It was a psychiatric hospital. The reason I chose to go there was because I knew the psychiatrist. As I recall, we spent most of the night there and your condition worsened. You started screaming uncontrollably and kicking anyone who got close to you. At one point it took all of us to hold you down. The doctor had to give you three separate injections to finally get you to sleep.

The "monster tranquilizer," as Aaron recorded in his journal, finally put me into a deep sleep. They carried me out to the car and drove through the night in an attempt to avoid morning traffic in Taipei.

Although the journals and memories of those involved all say I awoke after a day or so, my memories are very clouded. The next thing I remember is waking up in a bed in a very small and dark room. I opened my eyes and saw a strange man sitting on the bed. When he saw me looking at him, he smiled and said, "I'm President Horner, the Taipei Mission President. I'll be staying with you while President Watson gets everything ready for you to go home."

"Oh," I said and fell back asleep.

They originally planned to ask another missionary to return home early so he could accompany me on the plane. Instead, God made other arrangements. President Watson recalls,

A miracle occurred in getting Andy home. A church member who was doing business in Taiwan stopped by the mission home and asked if there was anything he could do to help. He had experience in administering medication by injection because someone in his family had diabetes. When he heard of Andy's situation, he volunteered to stay over for an extra day and take Andy home to the USA.

The next thing I remember is sitting on a bench that surrounded a planter at the airport and President Watson saying, "We just want to make sure you get home without any incident."

I agreed, and they gave me an injection. I remember walking down a narrow hallway. Turning around and looking back, I felt as if I had died and was leaving the world behind. President Watson and many missionaries stood behind a veil-like glass window, watching me walk away down a dark corridor.

The next time I woke up, I was on a plane sitting between two strangers. One was holding plastic flower cases. "We have these manufactured in Taiwan," the man said.

"Oh," I replied, and fell back to sleep.

Arriving in San Francisco, I remember hugging my parents. I was very confused why every time I tried to talk to my mom, she replied, "I don't speak Chinese. You have to speak in English." I kept trying to talk to her, but still she didn't understand. Finally, after everything I said, she would reply, "I don't know, but I love you."

Chapter 9
You're in a Hospital in Provo

"Mister Hogan, wake up!" [shake, shake] "Mister Hogan, get up!" [more shaking]

"Shemma maaa! (What!)" I cursed with my eyes still closed.

"Mister Hogan, wake up!"

Annoyed, I opened my eyes and through hazy vision saw a man dressed in hospital scrubs, squatting next to my bed, talking right in my face.

Forcing me to sit up he asked, "Do you know where you are?"

"What?" I said, rubbing my eyes, trying to focus.

"Do you know where you are?!"

I thought a minute. Looked around. Thought some more. Then, with a perplexed and disturbed voice admitted, "No."

"You're in a hospital in Provo, Utah," came the stabbing answer. "Are you feeling any side effects from the medication you're on?" he asked.

"I can't see clearly," I said.

"That will wear off as you wake up," he replied.

"My arm hurts," I said.

"That's from the IV. It will heal in a few days."

I fell back on the bed and the nurse walked out of the room, finally leaving me alone. "I can't be in Provo! I'm supposed to be in Chao Chou! What happened?" I wondered. The splotchy memories of my seemingly eternal ordeal felt like a dreary dream. However, in that moment the relief of a sane and calm mind felt as welcome to me as breath and freedom to a "caught and then released" fish.

"Zao an (good morning)!" laughed a voice next to me. I looked over to see another young man sitting up in a bed next to mine. I hadn't realized I had a roommate. "How does he know I speak Chinese?" I wondered.

"Hi," I replied. "Are you a missionary too?"

"Yes, I came here from Brazil for the same reason you came home from Taiwan, remember?"

"Oh," I said with a confused look on my face, wondering how he learned Mandarin in Brazil. I sat up and looked around my room for more discoveries. On a chair next to the phone, I found my leech book on top of a stack of several booklets of photos I had taken in Taiwan. I picked up the leech book and started flipping through all the pages of Chinese characters. On the last page I discovered someone else had written in English: "Things we want from America: Andy back. Doritos. Twizzlers." It was signed by Michael and Aaron.

"When did I ask them what they wanted me to send them from the states?" I wondered. I put the leech book down, picked up the photo books, and stared at the blurry memories, scarcely daring to think that my time in Taiwan as a missionary was over.

"Do you want to see my pictures from Taiwan?" I offered my roommate.

Annoyed, he shot back, "You've already shown me your stupid pictures a hundred times. I don't want to see them anymore."

"What?" I couldn't believe it. "How long have I been here?"

"Seven days."

I couldn't remember anything about being in the hospital for those seven days, but I figured it must be true if my roommate had heard me say zao an to him so many mornings that he memorized it.

As I ventured out of my bedroom, I found myself in a corridor where several other patients were coming out of their rooms. Some of them were older, some were middle aged, and a few looked about the same age as me. Without saying hello, I wandered to the far end of the hallway and looked out the window-to the world outside. It looked barren, cold, wet, and gray. I turned around and started walking to the other end of the hall. I passed a lounge area, a small room with chairs on all the walls, a nurse's station, and the bedrooms of the other patients. At last I came to a door at the other end of the hallway. I tried to open it but found the handle locked.

I wandered back to my bedroom, where breakfast waited near my bed. Not feeling very hungry, I picked at the pulpy pancakes and skipped over the syrup-soaked sausage. The nurse surprised me when he came to get my food tray. Rather than dump the leftovers in the garbage, he started picking through my food! After careful examination, he made notes of everything I ate and everything I left.

"Better get dressed," he said, as he carried the tray out of the room, "Group therapy starts in just a few minutes."

After everyone had gathered in the room with the chairs around the walls, each of us stood and said our names. The doctor was last.

"I'm Dr. Walker," he said. "Now, let's talk about this special section of the hospital and why you are all here. We lock the door at the end of the hallway to keep the world outside and so you can feel safe and secure inside," he explained. *"Some of you were brought here and some of you have chosen to come. The thing you all have in common is a rock in your shoe. When the rock first fell into your shoe you didn't stop to get it out. You shook your foot this way and you shook it that way. Eventually you learned to live with the pain. But the rock cut your foot and the wound got infected making it impossible for you to continue your walk of life. That's why you came to the hospital. Our purpose here is to help you to stop, take your shoe off, dump the rock out, wash the dirt out, then put a bandage on the cut, and allow you to start walking again."*

Thus my time at the hospital's Depression Center began. Over the next few days, I sat through many sessions of group therapy, trying to figure out just why this happened to me and how I should deal with it. Rather than look inward, I became convinced the "rock in my shoe" that had caused my breakdown was my parents.

In one session, the doctor challenged us to go to the person who "caused our depression" and tell him or her, "I am strong now and I'm not going to let you bother me anymore." Fearing the worst-that I might send Mother into mania and Dad into a temper tantrum-I told the doctor I needed to meet with my parents. He arranged a meeting and sat in as the referee. I remember spilling many tears as I criticized different things my parents had said and done during my growing up years.

"You said if I ever messed up in life that you failed as a parent and the sin would be on your head," I bawled at my mother.

"Every time I did something wrong, I was afraid that you would lose your temper. It made me feel like I always had to be perfect," I whined at my dad.

My parents listened quietly and spoke in the same soft tone that they had used throughout my childhood days when I had cried at their bedside. They humbly apologized and made no rebuttal.

Talking to my parents may have removed a grain of sand from my shoe, but the giant boulder of a chemical imbalance remained undetected—at least by me.

Journal Entry, 11/11/91, Provo, Utah

Well, as my time goes on in this loony bin, I'm learning more and more about myself and why this all happened. The things I've learned are pretty basic: 1. Everyone wants to be loved, including self by self. The other day I realized the only way to help others is to first help and love myself. Guess what? I found that I really do. I looked in the mirror and I told that punk I really do love him. Now I feel good about myself and I feel that I can start to help others again. While thinking about the triangle of truth, I forgot one main thing and that is that "man" has to love himself, too. It's so simple that it's almost funny. So now I feel ready to get back out and start helping others, but first I have to prove my sanity so they will let me out. In the meantime, I'm trying to enjoy my mission's "halftime" as Cris (my older brother) put it.

Oh, here's an interesting thing. The other day my parents gave me a letter that President Watson sent to them. Among other things it said, "Today I received a call from the missionaries in Chao Chou with some good news. They were visiting a church member who lives in the back of a hair dresser's shop. One of the customers, noticing that they were foreigners, commented that when she was in the post office that day the clerk had told her that someone had left a bag at the post office that must have belonged to a foreigner. The missionaries immediately went to the post office, and sure enough, it was Andy's bag. They indicated that his scriptures, dictionary, and camera were still in the bag, along with the address and phone book of all his contacts."

I guess I could say, "So, did I speak truth that if God wanted us to have it, it would turn up? Did I have truth?" I don't think anyone would listen to me now. I'm the one with the problem–dui bu dui (right)?

Rather than face the most obvious "truth" (that I was mentally ill), my bewildered brain chose to believe that "the truth triangle" was the real reason for the experience in Chao Chou. I felt different from the other patients. I thought they needed to be there, but for me, the hospital was just a vehicle God used to get me back to the States en route to a special, and important calling. At that time I didn't know what the word "chronic" meant. Even if I did, my stubborn mindset never would have allowed myself to admit mental illness was to become my permanent partner.

My mission "halftime" in the hospital lasted a whole month. To my surprise, for the most part, the time passed quite enjoyably. I was granted more freedom than in the mission field. The pressure of achieving my monster goals in Taiwan deflated. Visitors were allowed to see me from the very first day. After just a week, they allowed me to leave the hospital for accompanied activities. Sometimes my parents took me out to dinner or for a drive up Provo Canyon. Sometimes I went out on the town with the who were assigned to work in Provo. During the day I often went on long walks with Dr. Walker. In the evening, if I didn't have any plans, the hospital's Group Outing Specialist always had creative activities for any who wanted to participate.

These activities helped ease the culture shock of my unexpected "transfer" to America. However, nothing could have prepared me for the jolting wake-up call that rang through one night as I sat in my room writing letters to friends in Taiwan. I had received phone calls from my parents every night since I "came to." So when I picked up the receiver, an unexpected surprise greeted me. Instead of my mother's usual loud greeting, a quiet, gentle, and almost timid voice said, "Hello, Andy."

I recognized Dawn's voice and instantly my heart took flight like a flock of startled pigeons. "Your parents told me you were in the hospital and I wanted to call, see how you are doing, and tell you I love you."

Swallowing the huge lump of panic that flew up into my throat, and scarcely able to talk due to choked-up breathing, I told her I was fine and I loved her, too. As the conversation proceeded, she didn't pry for dreary details and she didn't press for eerie explanations. She only comforted and reassured me with careful words of cheer.

At one point, she said she loved me as much now as she had before and, though she didn't understand why all this happened, she believed it was for a purpose. Hearing her say this soothed my heart and pacified my mind.

Talking to Dawn and believing what happened to me in Chao Chou hadn't scared her away comforted me tremendously. It motivated me to face the challenge of getting out of the hospital and back to my mission with a positive attitude. The attitude I actually took, however, was still more denial than optimism.

As I jack-hammered out thoughts of reality, all Dr. Walker could do was try his best to direct me through the dust and keep me from falling into potholes of my self-destructive thinking. It took a little work, but eventually he convinced me to tell him about the secret list of goals I kept on the card in my scriptures. After listening to the long list, Dr. Walker tried to explain how these "unrealistic self expectations," as he called them, allowed pressure to pile up. Further, he said that by expecting to do the impossible, and only being satisfied with perfection, the only result I could ever expect was failure. "Too much pressure and constant feelings of failure are causes of depression and anxiety," he explained.

Dr. Walker then told me a story about another patient he had worked with who grew up on a farm. He said, like me, this young man also had "cock-a-doodle-do" expectations of himself. Trying to relate something in language the young farmer could understand, the doctor asked him if he could lift a baby calf off the ground and hold it in his arms.

"Of course," came the stout answer.

"How much weight would the calf put on in one day?" the doctor asked.

"Not much, maybe a pound or so is all," the young farmer answered.

"So you could lift the calf the next day?"

"Yes."

"And the next?"

"Yes."

"Could you lift the cow every day until it was full grown?"

Dr. Walker told me he couldn't help laughing when the boy told him he could probably lift a full-grown cow.

"Can you see how ridiculous and self destructive the poor kid's thinking was?" Dr. Walker asked.

I forced a laugh, but inwardly I felt as if the doctor was mocking me. It was as if someone told him my story about taking two seconds off my mile time each race until I held the state record. It trampled my pride that he could laugh at something so serious as the way my mind worked.

I still trusted him, however, and as the days passed we continued our walks and talks. You know how with some people you get so relaxed you say things and then later wish you hadn't? I guess I should have known. After all, he was a psychiatrist. But on those walks and talks, he had a way of making me feel that he was a friend who really cared.

In one of our conversations, I confided in him something I had never told anyone. I told him about my scary thoughts; specifically the urge I had felt as a youth to punch my math teacher in the sensitive spot. After I said it, I watched his eyes intensely to see what kind of a reaction he would have. Instead of telling me what I expected–that these thoughts came from the devil and I was just an innocent victim– he calmly said, "This only proves you are ill. Everyone who knows you knows you would abhor such thoughts and you would never carry them out as long as you were in your right mind."

The doctor meant the statement to be in my defense. I interpreted it to be enemy fire. The cannon ball that completely blew away our relationship happened a few days later when the doctor and I went for another walk. He mentioned something about the medical committee discussing my scary thoughts. "You told other people?" I screeched, like a signal flare calling all my emotions to the front line.

"Yes, I thought you knew there is a whole committee of medical professionals who discuss our findings from these walks and try to come up with the best medication and treatment for you," he defended.

"I thought we were friends!" I fired back. "You don't care about me, you're just doing your job and when I am gone you will forget me."

"I am your friend," he said with a shielded look in his eye. "I want what is best for you."

"Friends don't go around blabbing secrets about their friends to others," I said, fighting desperately to hold back the mounting tears.

No one likes to be told they are sick when they think they are not. When sick babies fuss, parents can put medicine in their bottles. When sick youth or adults fuss, it's impossible to force help on them. My childish reaction to Dr. Walker telling me I was ill was to stop trusting his knowledge and experience. Rather, I started to viciously hate him, and to blame him for my troubles.

After our battle of misunderstanding, I thought of myself as a prisoner of war who needed a secret strategy to get out of the concentration camp they had disguised as a hospital. I quit confiding the truth to Dr. Walker. I only told him what I thought he wanted to hear. I pretended to feel happy and good all the time. I didn't take to heart anything he said in group therapy sessions, but pretended to listen and participate intently. I overdid everything he asked me to and then exaggerated my reports by saying his therapy program helped tremendously. I told him his prescribed medication transformed me into a new person and I felt my mental strength returning in hulk-like leaps and bounds.

When Dr. Walker photocopied articles to help me understand my illness, I pretended to read them. However, instead of thinking about the words on the pages, my mind wandered far away, obsessing on two different theories or explanations of what "really" happened to me in Chao Chou.

The first theory was that God had placed me in a time warp. Nothing was real. When I came to understand and grasp the truth triangle and live it with perfect faith without any doubts or fear, then I would wake up in Chao Chou. Everything would be normal and the manic episode and Provo hospital would only be a bad dream—what I had prayed for while kneeling on the floor in the church.

The second theory was that I had, in fact, found God in Chao Chou. I imagined I had actually been taken into Jesus' presence and spent time with Him. When He sent me back to my body, Jesus, out of mercy, decided I wasn't ready for the responsibility of remembering my visit with Him. So, He blessed me with a horrible memory of the breakdown and made me forget being with Him until the next life.

I know. I know. How could I really believe these things? Please try to understand how real and damaging such a breakdown is to the person who experiences it. Even though I had "come out of it," I didn't have a textbook to explain the chemical spill-out in my brain that produced such chaos in thought and emotion. I guess such "a book" did exist. His name was Dr. Walker.

Until I acknowledged I had an illness it was impossible for Dr. Walker to help me. Lost in my monstrous mountain of denial, I found myself all alone, trying to make sense with a mind that was senseless. My two theories gave instant comfort and a numbing relief. They were much easier to accept than the painful reality that I had become the very thing I made fun of as a youth each time I joked, "You must be a loony!"

In addition to not listening to what the doctor tried to teach me about my illness, I also refused to learn about the medication I took. I didn't feel any different taking it and I didn't think I needed it. I must have feared that learning about it would convince me otherwise. I never even cared to look at the labels to learn the names of what I gulped down.

The only thing I noticed about the medication was that it invoked uncomfortable side effects. Sometimes I had to go outside and sprint up and down the parking lot to get the energy out of my legs. It felt the worst when I lay in bed trying to go to sleep. All the lights were out, and everyone else snored and slumbered, but my eyes stared at the ceiling as I flexed muscles in my legs trying to rid them of the irritating energy.

This bothered me so much that on one of our outings I told my parents about it. "That is called RLS (Restless Leg Syndrome)," they said. "There are drugs that can help get rid of it, or you can just work it out by getting a massage or flexing and relaxing your muscles." I decided to just work it out; the last thing I wanted was to tell the doctor I had a problem.

My medication's side effects hit me now and then, but the bigger bully, depression, constantly threw in punches. The two were a gang that loved to pick on me when they found me alone, with no activity to accompany my thoughts. Happily, many people rallied around me to help fight the incessant rumble, by providing meaningful activities to keep my mind away from these abusive thugs.

My parents made the hour-long trip nearly every day, just to take me out to dinner. After eating, I often joined up with the local missionaries as they searched out and fed the spiritually starved in

Provo. The sweetest activity of all was when I got to help interpret for a family of interested people from China.

During that time of teaching the Chinese mainlanders, Dr. Walker delivered a letter from Church Headquarters. He watched closely as I read the short and direct letter:

> *Dear Andy,*
> *This is to notify you that your mission assignment has been changed from the Taiwan Taichung Mission to the Montana Billings Mission. We appreciate your willingness to accept this assignment and are confident that you will be able to successfully fulfill this new calling.*

To be honest, the letter made my heart drop. With Dr. Walker studying my face, I tried not to show disappointment, but my expression must have been as obvious as a scolded dog on a tether line.

"I think we'd better have a talk," Dr. Walker said.

As he led me down the familiar sidewalk toward the fire hydrant on the corner, Dr. Walker tried desperately to get me to let it all out. "How do you really feel about going to Montana?"

"Fine," I muttered, trying to hold my emotions inside. I wanted to get out of the hospital and start doing "important" things so badly, I was willing to face what was one of my worst fears.

Before I sent in my mission application papers there were two places that scared me the most. First was the Orient...and second: an English speaking, stateside mission. When I received my assignment to Taiwan, the only consolation I could think of was, "Well, at least I won't have to worry about going to a stateside mission."

This letter made the impossible happen: I had to face not just one, but both of my worst mission assignment fears. It didn't enter my mind that, just like God taught me to love Taiwan and all Oriental people, He could also teach me to find joy serving the people of Montana. At that moment, my heart felt as if it had been frozen by a bitter cold wind that suddenly blew down from the north.

While I tried to get a grip on the icy shards of reality that were slicing through my mind, Dr. Walker interrupted, "I know you really wanted to go to a mission where you could use your Chinese. To be honest, I don't know if you are ready to leave the hospital. If you feel you can do it, I'll let you go. But, I'm afraid that you might end up right back here."

"I'll be fine," I promised.

I don't remember much about preparing to leave the hospital or saying goodbye to my family again. Really, the only thing I remember was my dad telling me he had spoken with my new mission president, President Condie, and a "special surprise" waited for me in Montana.

Chapter 10
Welcome to Helena (Hand Basket)

After take-off from Salt Lake City, the flight attendant barely had time to serve peanuts and soda pop before the captain announced the descent into Billings. At the airport, President Condie greeted me with a warm smile and a firm handshake. "This is your new companion Glen," he said pointing to a dark haired, freckled missionary who stepped forward and shook my hand with a friendly gleam in his eye and smile on his face.

Remembering that point in our missions, Glen Olson recalls:

When I first heard from President Condie that I would be the new companion for a mission transfer missionary with a mental illness I fought with several emotions. First was the willingness to be patient, kind, understanding, and help Andy make a smooth transition to Montana. Second was the apprehension of serving as companion to a missionary with a mental illness.

President Condie did not tell me much information about Andy's condition other than "he had a bit of a problem–a mental breakdown in Taiwan." These are the words I remember. I had no past experience with mental illness. My preconceived notions were, for lack of gentler terms, "a zit-faced introvert who could barely take care of himself." I was somewhat nervous about my new companion.

Meeting Andy for the first time, my ideas were challenged immediately. He was polite, personable and looked as normal as the all-American boy. Over the next several weeks the only indications that Andy had any trouble at all were his stories and recollections of the breakdown in Taiwan, along with the medication he took daily. The medications seemed to sedate or "mellow him out some." But, for all I could tell he was intelligent, motivated, related well with people, and could even play missionary basketball.

In the days that followed I quickly picked up on the high status Glen held within the mission. It didn't take long to realize he was the one they sent the "troubled" missionaries to. He was a hard worker. He kept the mission rules. He was always positive and patient. He taught the missionary discussions knowledgeably and effectively. He was loved by the mission president and respected by the other missionaries. Glen was the missionary I had been when I moved to Chao Chou. Now, I wasn't just a greenie all over again, I was also a missionary with issues.

Like a snowplow in a sleet storm, thoughts of my crash from "super" missionary to "special" missionary sloshed over my ego and shoved me deep into the gutter of depression. It never occurred to me that this incredible low was compounded by an illness. Rather, I interpreted it as my body being shipped to Montana while my heart still throbbed in Taiwan.

The more I dwelt on the differences between the two missions, the more depressed I felt. In a desperate effort to hold on to the past, I surrounded myself with everything Chinese. I wore my Chinese nametag so people would ask me about it. I made my companion eat at Chinese restaurants. I always carried a tape recorder, and spoke Chinese into it as I made voice tapes to Yoner, Ken, friends in Chao Chou, and anyone else I could think of in Taiwan who "needed" to hear from me. I studied my Chinese scriptures and discussions. I even wrote parts of my weekly reports to President Condie in Chinese.

Glen was very patient and understanding. Still, during our time together I suffered depression more heavily than I had ever felt it before. The days were short and cold. The nights were long and cold. My emotions felt as chilled and heavy as the big, Montana nighttime sky.

After just a week or two with Glen, the mission office held a big dinner for all the county missionary leaders in the mission. Glen, who was a leader for the Billings area, told me he would go to the dinner and then meet me at the church for the leaders-versus-junior-companions basketball game. This was the "big surprise" my dad had spoken of when we said goodbye at the airport. He thought being able to play basketball would lighten my mind and lift my heart. He didn't realize I didn't care about basketball anymore.

Somehow, in the shuffle of preparation, Glen couldn't find a church member or another missionary to "baby-sit" me while he attended the dinner. So, I got to tag along. During the dinner, I tried to keep to myself and not get in the way of the "big-wig" county leaders. There must have been some whispering going on because, as I sat there eating, someone came over and tapped me on the shoulder. I looked up to see a smiling missionary standing over me. He held out his hand and said, "I'm Ryan. I heard you came here from Taiwan and that you speak Mandarin. Is this true?"

"Yes," I answered with intrigue.

"I am the county leader up in Helena," he continued, "and we've been having trouble communicating with some Chinese friends who are students at the local college. Would you be willing to come help us teach them?"

A chorus of angels couldn't have sounded more appealing to my ears than these words. "Heavens yes!" I almost screamed. The rest of the evening and the next couple of days floated by. For the first time, a ray of sunlight pierced the gloom that clouded my view of this reassigned mission.

Before I left Billings, President Condie called me in for an interview. "As you go to Helena to work with the Chinese students I want you to remember one thing." He paused to make sure he had my undivided attention and then continued, "When an airplane takes off, it doesn't shoot straight up into the sky; it gradually gains altitude. As you continue your mission in Helena, I want you to do the same. Climb slowly so you don't stall and crash."

As Ryan drove toward my new area, President Condie's words repeated over and over in my mind like the streaking yellow lines that divided the northbound and southbound lanes of the highway. The more I tried to figure out what "slowly gaining altitude" meant, the more perplexed I felt. Finally, I decided to get a second opinion.

"Hey, Ryan," I started. "President Condie and I had an interview before I left. He says I'm an airplane trying to take off, and if I try to launch straight up, I won't go anywhere except crashing down. He says I should gain altitude gradually. Do you think that means I should only follow some of the rules and do missionary work just some of the time?"

Ryan laughed, "I don't know about that. I think he means you should relax a little and not try to do everything perfectly all at once."

"So it's okay to break the rules every now and then?" I questioned.

"I'm not going to say it. You have to decide for yourself," he concluded.

As we exited Interstate 15 into Helena, snowflakes were flickering in the lights of the capitol building that shone down the hillside to where my new companion waited at the church house. As soon as we stopped in the parking lot, he walked over, opened my door, and thrust out his hand.

"Howdy! I'm Blake. Can I help you get your luggage? Cool name tag! Can you really read that?" His smiling face beamed with more brilliance than all the capitol building lights-including the flagpole spotlight.

We met with the two Chinese students once a week, and though I truly enjoyed and, in fact, lived for those meetings, I quickly realized the bulk of our time would be spent finding and teaching the Helena locals. This realization set in like freezing drops of an icicle falling down the back of my neck from an uncovered porch. I truly believe God sent me to be Blake's companion to see me through the chilliest and darkest days of my life thus far.

Each morning he got up at the appointed hour, 6:30, got dressed, and tromped outside our little cottage into the frozen darkness to chop firewood. He hauled the wood inside and used it to start a roaring fire in the stove that sat in the living room. (We did have one electric heater that burned all night between our two beds and kept us fairly warm as long as we kept ourselves buried under the thick covers.) Only when the fire heated the house comfortably, would I drag myself out of the bedroom and into the living room. Together we would kneel for our morning companionship prayer. After saying amen, I'd pull up a blanket and my Chinese scriptures, lie on the couch in front of the stove, read a verse or two, and then fall sound asleep.

For our first few days together, I tried to get up on time but never found the strength to stay awake. I didn't realize it was the medication I took before bed that knocked me out cold. I just thought I had become weak in mind. Following failed attempts to wake up, I began to realize it was impossible to be the same missionary I had been in Taiwan. This realization, pushed by the excuse of "gradually gaining altitude," started a snowball of changes in my missionary lifestyle.

I started writing letters, doing wash, and other personal things on days other than P-day. I broke another mission rule by listening to worldly music. I rationalized it to be okay because it wasn't full-blown rock and roll, but Chinese pop I had purchased in Taiwan.

This relaxed attitude about keeping the rules made mission life much easier than in Taiwan—at least it took away the pressure of living up to mammoth expectations and monster goals. I also felt justified because for every gouge of guilt that inevitably followed each rule breaking, I had the soothing saying of "Don't try to take off straight up."

Over the next few weeks, my angle of take-off fell lower and lower. "Out the door to do missionary work at 9:30" plunged to "out the door after lunch." "Eating dinner at a church member's house" sometimes dropped to "hanging out at the church members' house all evening." When Blake suggested, "Let's go meet some new people and try to set up some teaching appointments with the extra time we have because of a discussion cancellation," I returned with, "No, let's go get our groceries so we don't have to waste P-day time shopping."

Little by little, I started letting down my discipline. If it weren't for a previously scheduled appointment, this casualness could have cost my life. The event happened one day when Ryan asked Blake and me if we wanted to go cut Christmas trees with some church members from their area. "Sure!" I exclaimed. But Blake, looking at his schedule, reminded me we already had a teaching appointment scheduled for that time.

I remember walking through the door just after returning home from our appointment. The phone started ringing. Blake answered in his regular cheery mood. "What?" He paused and slowly sat down. "Okay, I'm sitting down." His expression changed from joyous to jaundiced. "When? How? Where? How are the others?" After many long pauses and a few more questions, he quietly hung up the phone.

"What's up?" I asked.

"I think you'd better sit down to hear this," he solemnly answered. I slumped down on the couch. With tears welling up in his eyes Blake explained, "Ryan died today. Remember how he asked us if we wanted to go cut Christmas trees? After the activity with the members, Ryan, his companion, and two other missionaries decided to go back and cut a tree for their house. When they drove into the mountains, they found an old mining cave with a gate in front of it. There was a small space between the top of the gate and the roof of the cave. All four of them climbed the gate and squeezed through the space. Without any lights they felt their way along the cave. Ryan led the group, and all of a sudden he was gone. The other missionaries yelled for him and felt around, but he wasn't there. In terror they ran back to the car and called the police. When the search and rescue team went into the cave, they discovered Ryan had fallen about 70 feet down into a chasm. He survived the fall but died of shock and exposure before they could get him out."

The next day we attended a special meeting with President Condie and the other missionaries in our county. The three missionaries who went in the cave with Ryan came, too. They were crying, sobbing, and holding hands, as if they were still in the dark and would lose each other if they let go.

I remember Ryan's companion speaking to the missionaries of our county, begging, pleading with us to follow all the rules. "If we had kept the rules, Ryan would still be with us and I would still have a companion," he said in between sniffles and eye wipes.

Seeing the grief and agony of those three missionaries strongly emphasized to me that I needed to be careful as I searched for the balance between "taking off straight up" and "nose-diving into the runway." I knew if we had chosen to go with them, with my mindset of "It's okay to break the rules," I wouldn't have had the courage to say no to climbing that gate and blindly exploring the cave.

With his passing, Blake and I started working with Ryan's Chinese students all by ourselves. It turned out that neither of them had bundles of interest. Theirs was more of a curiosity to learn about "western religion," as they called it, and they enjoyed the novelty of a Mandarin-speaking American. They introduced us to their friends who also started coming to our meetings. However, it wasn't long before their amusement with my language ability faded away, as did their interest in religion. Soon, all but one quit meeting with us. Once again, Blake and I found ourselves with little to do except knock on the doors of the locals.

Slowly, as the weeks dragged into months, and following the example of my wonderful and patient senior companion, I began to show heart in my service for the people of Helena. I still clung to Taiwan and couldn't let go of Chinese things, but at the same time, I found a desire to help and love the people of my new mission. Blake and I shared several uplifting experiences.

In addition to assisting other people's lives, I also started to see change for the better in my own life. I remember one particular discussion with Dafne, the lone remaining Chinese student who was still interested in meeting with the missionaries. While asking me a question about a passage of scripture she had read, she said a word that I didn't understand. Rather than pretend I understood, I did something I had never found courage to do since I had started learning Chinese. I held up my hand motioning her to stop talking and said, "Dwei bu qi, wo ting bu dong (I'm sorry, I didn't understand)". It was amazing to see that she didn't think less of me for the admission, but rather, she was happy that I wanted to understand her question in full.

Other changes for the better happened. With our successes, I started to feel accepted and respected by my fellow missionaries. Like the warm rays of sunshine that lasted a little longer each day, my self-confidence also started to return. I came to realize that stateside missions weren't so bad after all. The joy of missionary work was possible to feel even in the midst of dark and freezing Montana winters.

When word of Blake's transfer and my assignment as senior companion arrived, I received it as a pat on the back and a vote of confidence in my leadership ability. With the transfer, President Condie not only promoted me to senior companion but made me a trainer as well!

As I waited at the church for the van to arrive with my new greenie I felt poised, prepared, and powerful. "So powerful," I thought, "I won't need my pitiful pills anymore."

When the van pulled up I walked over, opened the door and peered inside. "Hello, I'm Andy, your trainer. Welcome to Helena!"

"Yo dude! Wha'sup?" he replied with a heavy east-coast surfer dude accent. "I'm Johnny."

I wasn't positive, but in the faint light of the van, I thought I saw a hole in his left earlobe where an earring had recently been removed.

We loaded up and started driving toward our apartment. On the way, we passed a field with cows standing next to the roadside fence. Johnny yelled out, "Mooers!" Quickly he rolled down his window, stuck his head out, and bellowed at the long-eyed Holsteins, "Moo!"

"This guy will keep our companionship interesting," I thought to myself. "With his fun-loving spirit and my serious and solemn mentality, maybe we can do some balanced work together. By sending me Johnny, President Condie has given me an opportunity to really shine. I've got to do it right this time."

On our first morning together, with great difficulty, I forced myself out of bed at 6:30 and called Johnny to companionship study. Thinking of the truth triangle, I chose charity for our topic. "If we can develop charity, or in other words, the pure love of Christ, then our missionary work will take off. We won't have to worry about stats because the numbers will just come naturally. We won't have to waste our time looking for interested people, because they will come searching for us. When they feel God's love, they will bring their loved ones into the light as well. This is truth, and it is the secret to success in missionary work," I said in conclusion.

Not having any scheduled appointments that day I decided to take Johnny out on the town to try to meet some new people. I thought with his greenie attitude and fresh faith, our chances of finding an interested person might improve ever so slightly. We drove to a trailer-house neighborhood, parked the car, and walked to the closest door. I knocked and gave the approach, "Hello, we are missionaries. I'm Andy and this is Johnny. Would you be interested in hearing a message about Jesus Christ and His plan of happiness?"

There was a short pause before the man answered. Expecting the usual rejection, it threw me completely off guard when he said, "Yes, I am interested, but I can't talk right now. Can you come back this evening?"

"S-s-sure," I stammered, pulling out my empty schedule. "Will 7:00 work for you?"

"That will be fine. See you then," he said, closing the door. As we walked toward the next trailer house, I said to Johnny, "Wow! First try and boom, we get a score! You get to do the next door."

Johnny knocked.

A lady in silky, blue pajamas, looking as if we woke her up, answered the door. Johnny gave his approach and asked if she would be willing to hear our message.

"Yeah, I've been fixin' to talk with y'all. Can y'all come back this evening?" My jaw about hit the gravel, but Johnny didn't seem the least bit surprised. Without missing a beat, he pulled out his schedule and set an appointment for 8:00. After she shut her door and we were out of hearing range, I yelled out, "Tai bang le!"

"And what does that mean?" asked Johnny.

"It means it's too good to be true," I answered. Two appointments in one day!

Johnny looked at me as if I was the greenie. "Yeah? So? Isn't that the way it's supposed to happen?"

"Yes, it's the way it's supposed to happen, but it usually doesn't happen that way. I've been here for two months, talked with everyone I could, and have only found a small handful of interested people. Now, here we are nabbing two appointments right in a row!" I exclaimed. "You are good luck."

"Dude, didn't you say if we have charity for the people, success will find us? I took it you were teaching me truth."

"Yeah, you're right," was all I could say.

That evening at 7:00 sharp we returned for our scheduled appointment. Knocking on the door, we found no one home. "It was too good to be true," I thought. Turning to Johnny, I said, "Well, let's go see if the lady at our 8:00 appointment is home and ask if she can see us now."

We tromped across the way and knocked on the door. The same lady, looking much more awake and alive answered. "Didn't y'all schedule for 8:00?"

"Yes, we did, but we had an appointment with your neighbor at 7:00 and he wasn't home. So, we came over to see if you could meet now."

"Yes, I can. Come on in," she said with a cautious smile. We went in the house and she introduced herself, Shannon, a single mom with three children.

Like Zhong in Chao Chou, Shannon turned out to be "golden" as well. She had an incredible desire to find answers to her spiritual questions. We met with her often, and though her progression and acceptance was slow, when it came, it came with conviction and dedication.

Through this time, Johnny and I worked diligently. We followed the mission rules most of the time. We did everything we could to find success. Pretty soon the number of interested people we found tripled. It was wonderful to spend more of our time teaching and serving our new friends and less time introducing ourselves to people who weren't interested.

As time went on, Johnny's and my friendship and trust grew immensely. I started opening up to him. I told him about how I came to Montana after thinking too deeply about spiritual things in Taiwan. Still in denial that I had a mental illness, I made it sound like what happened in Taiwan was a spiritual experience, not a mental breakdown. Sadly, this denial, a lack of medication, and the deep conversations stirred up the steaming symptoms of extreme mania. In the darkness of my mind, and blind to my illness, all I could see was an approaching light of what I deemed to be spirituality. When I heard the symptomatic whistle blows, I covered my ears and started sprinting down the emotional tracks straight toward the approaching locomotive.

Journal Entry, 3/17/92 Helena, Montana
I'm back! I haven't written in my journal for a long time and I need to get caught up. The first bit of news is that Dawn decided to go on a mission and she is now a Christian soldier working in Italy! It's pretty wild to think that she is really on a mission, but I wrote her a letter and told her if that's what she wants to do, then I support her 100%. It's going to be hard waiting that much longer for her, but I'm willing to do it.
Lately I've been dwelling on a few things that I was thinking about in Taiwan. Last Sunday I had a long talk with my companion, Johnny, about truth. I told him the things that I had been thinking about in Taiwan and how they led to a fenged out (Chinglish for "crazy") missionary. He listened

intently and wanted to discuss it more. We talked late into the night about "what is truth" and "how we can gain a full realization of it."

I told him that everyone is looking for one characteristic of God or another; be it happiness, success, acceptance, healing, peace, comfort, or anything else that is good. In their quest for these things, what people don't realize is that thing they really are looking for ultimately, is always God.

God is the source of every good thing. In order to believe in God, or at least, to believe that the God we teach them about is true, they need to feel love. I told Johnny that when we have charity, or the pure love of Christ, for the people we work with, we become a part of truth and are able to help them find what they are looking for to solve their problems.

After talking with Johnny, now once again, I find myself searching. Do I have this love? Can I live according to the knowledge of this truth? Since I came home from Taiwan, I have done what everyone told me: "Just don't think about it." All this time I haven't dared to look back, to search or even think about these things. I felt as if I had searched too deeply, and by doing so I lost Taiwan. Well, I'm thinking again. I'm searching again, and am willing to try again.

As I thought about the truth triangle more and more the obsessive thoughts plowed over reality and again, pressed my mind into insanity. One night, shortly after writing the above journal entry, Johnny and I went to a discussion with Dafne, and her friend who was visiting from China.

Since the discussion was all in Chinese, I had a mask and could speak without worrying about what my companion would think. We got into deep religious philosophy and by the end of the discussion my mind was racing through space like a satellite blown out of orbit.

Remember how I said mania feels sensational at first? The high that night made me feel like a shooting star flying high above the earth granting wishes and spreading wonder for everyone below me. Dafne and her friend were also blinded by the manic floodlight. To them I looked brilliant, energetic, and deeply spiritual. How could they know I wasn't a star to place wishes on, but rather a streaking satellite crashing toward a rocky reality.

When we arrived home, long after mission curfew, the phone rang. It was Dafne. She wanted to talk some more. Johnny went to bed. I stayed up late into the night and early into the morning talking to her about my manic philosophies of truth.

Chapter 11
The Second Breakdown

To describe the events of my second breakdown, I thought it would be interesting to hear it from an outside-looking-in view, a view from the eyes of my incredible companion. The following is John Robertson, my dear greenie, telling his version of my second breakdown:

Well, I decided to just start from the beginning of the best part of the story and tell it as I remember it. A few things I should say about the events leading up to the infamous Bozeman trip. Andy Hogan had talked with me about his theories on truth, and to be honest, he had me convinced that he knew what he was talking about. Even if I really didn't understand it fully, it sure seemed that he believed what he was saying. I mean we had a great friendship and, well, I liked the guy. I was happy to have him as a companion. He told me all sorts of stories about the people he met in Taiwan and how he fell in love with the people he taught. It all sounded like what a mission was supposed to be.

Anyway, we had taught some great people in Helena, and I was happy with our success. One person we were teaching was a Chinese girl who went to the local college. That day, Andy said he wanted to go visit her and talk to her about some concerns she and a friend were having. We were in the recreational room of the dorm building, and Andy spoke with the girls in Chinese while I sat quietly and smiled. Every now and then they would look over at me and I would grin and say, "ting bu dung," (no idea if I spelled that right), meaning, "I don't understand." They would chuckle and go right back to their conversation. We left the college and made our way back to our house. On the drive Andy told me how the conversation went. We talked about their concerns.

As soon as we got in the house, the phone was ringing. Andy picked it up and started speaking Chinese. I determined that the girls were on the phone, and since I could be of no help to the conversation, I just started my preparations for bed. I waited up until kinda late, but Andy was still talking on the phone when I dozed off.

The next morning was a multi-county missionaries training conference in Bozeman. I always liked the big conferences because they were a break from our everyday routine and I had a chance to see some other mission buddies. Since this was only my second month out. I was eager to see some guys from my MTC group and was raring to go. Andy, on the other hand, was still in bed when I was dressed. I nagged at him like an old bitty, and he finally crawled out of bed and into the shower. After we were both dressed and in the car, we hurried on our way to pick up another set of missionaries, Trent and his companion Hodges, or Hodgie as we called him. Hodgie was only a month older than me in the mission. You could say that we were both still greenies.

I remember going into their apartment. Andy sat down on their couch and almost fell asleep right there. Can't say that I thought anything was wrong because Andy usually dragged around like a tired old man in the mornings. Hey, some of us aren't cut out for this early morning stuff. We finally took off to the conference, just a bit later than we had planned, but we thought we still had plenty of time as long as Andy drove the way he usually did.

As we got into the car, Trent pulled out a radar-detecting device and handed it to Andy saying, "This is to help you remember how fast you are driving." Andy laughed, took it, and hung it on his visor.

The trip was pretty routine until we got about a half hour away from Bozeman. We had been talking and laughing and having a good time. No one thought anything was wrong with Andy, even though he had been silent for several minutes. All of a sudden he took his foot off the accelerator and slowed down to about 50 miles per hour. Now, keep in mind that this was 1992 before they took the speed limits off of the highways in Montana. So there were actually speed limit signs posted.

I think Trent was the first to say, "Umm, Hogan, what are you doing, man? My grandmother drives faster than this."

Andy simply replied, "I'm obeying the law."

"Well that's great, I'll give you a cookie when we get to the county missionaries conference. Now speed it up. We're going to be late as it is!"

We all kinda laughed and brushed it off, but Andy didn't speed up. We all started to comment and pass jokes but Andy never sped up. The comments and jokes got a bit rude, and still no reaction from Andy.

Trent was fuming and really starting to lose his cool, but still nothing from Andy. It wasn't until Trent screamed out, "What is your fetching problem?" that Andy finally reacted.

Andy said, "Isn't it ironic that as missionaries we ask people to change and accept new ideas, but we aren't willing to repent and change ourselves? Trent, the law says that I should not drive over 55 miles per hour. It's hard to keep it right on 55, so I'll just keep it at 50. That way I know that I'll always be obeying the speed limit. I have to obey the law of the land. The mission president and other leaders would want us to follow the law even if it means being a little late."

I think it was something in his voice, or just the way his face looked like a robot when he said this that made me think something was seriously wrong with Andy. I turned around and looked at Trent in the back seat. Neither one of us were smiling. Hodgie, on the other hand, was laughing. We both gave him the evil eye, and his face dropped. "What?" he asked innocently.

I asked Andy if he was all right and he said, "I've never been better. This time I found it. I really found it, and I'm not going to lose it." He continued to talk to me and say that things were good and he made a few interesting observations about the way Trent was acting. Then he said the one thing that let me know we were in for a ride. "Johnny, I think Trent needs to find TRUTH."

After more arguing between Trent and Andy, we finally came to the Bozeman exit off of the highway. We made a circle around the exit ramp and came up on the main street. Suddenly, Andy stopped talking and pulled off the side of the road right in front of a high school.

He cut the car off and turned around in his seat to face Trent. Needless to say Trent was livid by now. "What are you doing, man? We're almost there!"

Andy said, "Trent, it's time you found truth."

Trent screamed in anger and demanded that Andy give him the keys to the car. Andy took them out of the ignition and dropped them on the floor. "Not until you find truth."

I grabbed Andy's hand and turned him to face me. "Tell me, Hogan. Tell me all you know about truth." Hey, I know it sounds cheesy, but I figured that I could keep my cool while Trent and Hodgie found a way to get him out of the driver's seat.

Then I heard two car doors slam shut. I looked back and saw no one. They had ditched out on me!!! Left me there with this crazy guy and I had no freekin' clue where I was. All I knew was that I was in the middle of

111

*Montana and my home was on the other side of the world. Ok, so that's what
it felt like. The big sky country looked very big to me now.*

It turned out that Trent and Hodgie didn't "ditch" out on us.
Trent knew where the Bozeman missionaries' apartment was. They
broke into the apartment and called for help. During this time, my
reality flew farther and farther away. I became convinced Johnny was
God. At first Johnny tried to get me to snap out of it. When he saw
this wouldn't work, he started playing along, pretending to be God. It
was the only way I would listen to him and do what he asked. In a deep
booming voice, he ordered me to stay in the car while he made a phone
call.

The situation at the time was frantic. Now, however, it's rather
funny to think about John using his lowest, bass voice and commanding
me to "stay". John and I laugh about it now. You can too.

He couldn't get an answer at the churches listed in the phone
book at a payphone across the street, so he came back to the car. Using
his deep voice again, Johnny commanded me to give him the keys and
let him drive. He drove to a convenient store. It was there that the
mission president's assistants found us. Not realizing the severity of my
situation and the desperate need I had for medication, they took us
to the church house where the conference was being held. They told
Johnny to go into the meeting, and not tell anyone what was going
on.

By this point I could not reason or listen to reason. I sat down
outside and grabbed the handrail next to the steps. I refused to let go
for over an hour-even though it was cold and snowing. Glen, who was
now one of mission president's assistants stayed with me the whole
time trying to talk me into going inside.

President Condie was also attending the conference. Hearing
that I had been outside for so long, he gathered five or six of the
strongest missionaries and forced me into the building. I didn't go
willingly. I fought and screamed the whole way. All the missionaries in
the conference heard the noise.

They carried me inside and set me on a couch in the foyer. After a
while, I laid my head back on the couch, closed my eyes and pretended
to be asleep. I couldn't sleep, but the president and other missionaries
thought I was asleep. As I listened to whispers around me, I believed

I had died and was waiting to get into heaven. Glen later told me that in the conference, rumors spread like a Montana dust-devil that Andy was possessed with an evil spirit.

After a long while, I opened my eyes. Seeing my county leader there, I thought he was Christ. Bursting into tears I dropped to my knees and tried to kiss his feet. They pulled me back onto the couch. My mind worsened with each passing minute. President Condie called my parents and then asked for Johnny to come talk to them. John recalls,

Sean, one of the mission president's assistants pulled me out of the conference and told me Andy's parents were on the phone and they wanted to talk to me. I told them the whole story and answered a slew of questions. However, the one that seemed to be the most important, I couldn't answer. Mrs. Hogan asked if Andy was taking his medicine every morning.

"He keeps his pills in the bathroom and takes them when he gets out of the shower," I answered. "I'm never in there when he is. So, I'm not real sure if he's been taking them." They quickly determined that Andy had stopped taking his medicine and this breakdown was the result.

President Condie and Andy's parents decided what to do. President Condie made arrangements for Andy to go home that evening. Me and two other missionaries were to take him to the airport in Bozeman and accompany him to Salt Lake City. There his parents would pick him up at the airport. We would spend the night in a hotel in Salt Lake and come back on the first flight the next morning. I guess some circumstances require drastic measures.

President Condie then instructed us to watch over Andy while the President addressed the rest of the missionaries in the conference and let them know what was going on.

It sounded like an easy plan, but just getting Andy into the car was a major ordeal! He clawed, scratched and fought the whole way. The airport wasn't too far away from the church. None of us really knew exactly where it was. So, we took a long round-about way trying to find it. We went right through the center of town and Andy steadily got worse. He mumbled in Chinese. He spit on one of the missionaries sitting next to him. He yelled out the window in Chinese at an Asian man who was standing on the corner. He had fits of hysterical laughter immediately followed by bitter crying. We were all pretty freaked out.

Finally, we made it to the airport. We waited in the car for President Condie to come let us know what we needed to do. After his brief instructions we carried Andy into the airport and set him down in a wheelchair that was

at the front entrance. Suddenly Andy started spewing out swear words. Sean tried to cover up his mouth, but he wouldn't stop. Someone complained and the pilot came to investigate. When the pilot saw Andy, he told President Condie, "That man may not fly on my plane."

Okay, great. So what to do now? We dragged Andy back to the car and President Condie contacted Andy's parents. They decided it would be in Andy's best interest to take him to the hospital to try and get him medicated so he could fly home.

At the hospital emergency room, we were instructed to take Andy to a private room. I told the doctor everything that had happened. The doctor told us that Andy would have to be admitted and stay the night there. He called for two orderlies to go into the room and prepare Andy for the night. Then he asked everyone except President Condie and Glen to leave the room. Glen later told us the doctor told President Condie that Andy was "in for a very long recovery." He said that "it may take years, and sometimes people in this condition are never normal again."

Glen and President Condie came out and asked us to all gather around. "Go home," he said. "There is nothing more we can do for him. The doctors are going to get him medicated, and his parents are going to drive up tonight to pick him up. Everyone go home and remember the Hogans in your prayers."

All of a sudden the doors of the room where we had left Andy flew open. The two orderlies were on either side of him, escorting him out of the room. He looked from one orderly to the other, speaking in Chinese. I could hear one orderly talking back to him in a soft soothing voice saying things like, "All right then. You don't say. Wow, that's great. Yes sir, everything's gonna be just fine."

As they walked down the hallway we could see that they had replaced Andy's clothes with one of those nice little hospital gowns that don't exactly close in the back. All we could see was them disappearing down the hallway with his bare rear-end hangin' out of the hospital gown. He stopped talking for a second or two, then looked up at one orderly and asked in the most serious voice, "Do you feel a draft?" Everyone laughed, but with heavy hearts. President Condie's wife shook her head and said, "That poor, poor boy."

As I turned to leave and realized I was alone, suddenly the reality of the day's events and Andy's situation hit me like a ton of bricks. My companion and friend was going home because of a serious mental illness! It just didn't seem right. This wasn't supposed to happen to him. He was too good of a missionary, too good of an example, and too good of a friend. For the first time I felt that there was nothing I could do to help him. I wasn't feeling much like God any more.

After what felt like hours and hours of sleep, and with a feeling of exposed embarrassment, as if I had been hanging out in private places, I opened my eyes. "Where is Johnny?" I wondered. Looking around, my thoughts continued, "Where the heck am I?" Further examination showed I was locked in a small, square room with pale, yellow walls about the length of the mat on the floor that I had been sleeping on. A small, metal toilet sat on the other side in the corner, and a security camera hung from the ceiling. My clothes were folded neatly in a pile at the base of the mat, and a door with no handle, that looked as massive as a dungeon drawbridge, loomed over my head at the front of the mat. A sore rear end told me that they had used a sedative injection to gain control and put me to sleep.

Thinking back, I vaguely remembered my horrendous ordeal. "Oh, no!" I thought. "Not again!" Splotchy scenes of panic, profanity, unrepressed emotions, physical force, and impulses of rudeness flashed through my mind as if I were remembering a nightmare. "It couldn't have been a dream if I'm locked up in a loony bin," I mumbled.

I stood up and looked through the tiny window toward the top of the door. Down the hallway, at a nurse's station, stood my mom and dad! The nurse saw me peering through the window and said something to my parents. They spun around and came running over. Bursting through the door, they started hugging me as if I had just come back from the dead. Even though I was awake and appeared normal, the hospital people wouldn't let me out of the cell.

That night I again slept on the mat, and Dad slept on the tile floor next to me. I remember being woken up in the middle of the night to see a nurse standing there with a needle in her hand. I must have given some resistance, because the nurse said, "Please take it, I'm the only one here." Still I refused.

"Will you take it for me?" asked my dad.

Still believing the truth triangle was causing the experience, and willing only to do God's will, I queried my dad, "Who are you?"

"I think you know the answer to that question," he replied. I looked at his tired, concerned face for a moment. The love I saw overpowered the confusion in my mind and I nodded my head in agreement. Pulling up my hospital gown, I took the shot in the behind and fell back asleep.

When I finally got up the next day, Dad said he was flying home with me and I needed to get dressed. Wow, it felt good to put clothes on! I suppose it's standard protocol for hospitals to put their patients in hospital gowns, but for me suffering from severe mania, it only amplified the feeling of exposure and embarrassment.

After arriving at the airport in Salt Lake City, my parents drove me straight to a regional institute for behavioral medicine. The lady at the front desk pulled out an enlistment form. As Dad started filling out the form, Mother asked the lady what kind of program they would be putting me in. Like a drill sergeant she recited the schedule: "They're up at 6:00 for breakfast. Group sessions go from 7:00 to noon. After lunch they have class and intensive therapy. Bedtime at 8:30 is strictly enforced."

"Will he be allowed to sleep in if he needs to?" My mother asked with quiet concern.

"Sure," the lady replied. "We'll let him sleep until 7:00 on the first day." By this time, I was on the verge of tears and shaking with fear. It felt as if I was being checked into a concentration camp, not a healing institute. Worst of all, I had no say in the matter. My judgment and opinions were not even considered–at least not by the hospital people.

Mother, however, knew exactly what I needed. Turning her back to the lady, she took the clipboard from my dad, ripped up the pages and threw them on the counter. Then, looking tenderly into my eyes she said, "Andy doesn't need this. Let's go home."

I have often thought about how easy it would have been for my parents to just check me into that institution and let the professionals handle my case. I'm convinced if I had stayed there, I would have gotten a lot worse before I got any better.

My parents didn't take the easy way out. Instead, they were sensitive to my feelings and needs. As we walked out the door and started driving home, a mountain of love and gratitude for my mother and father filled my heart. I finally understood that the love they had expressed to me since childhood was true.

During my time at home, I relaxed and enjoyed the break from mission pressures. But I still felt I needed to go back and finish. A month later I called President Condie and asked if I could come back. He told me I would be assigned to go back to Helena and resume my duties as senior/trainer companion with Johnny...if I promised to take my medication.

My dad drove the eight-hour trek to take me back to Helena. We picked up Johnny and his new companion, Rubin, at our old apartment. Driving into town, we dropped off Rubin with his reassigned companion. Not wanting to leave, Dad offered to take Johnny and me out to dinner. After a nice dinner together, Dad drove us back to our pad where we hugged goodbye.

After Dad had reluctantly driven away, Johnny and I started talking about the funny, no, crazy events of the breakdown. Still in denial that mental illness caused the breakdown, I looked Johnny in the eye and in a very serious tone said, "You know, I think that some of the things I said and did were pretty profound and we should learn from them."

"Dude, you were totally whacked," Johnny said flatly. Not wanting to argue, I changed the subject. "What happened with Shannon?"

He hesitantly replied, "Rubin decided to drop her because she wasn't showing progress. We haven't seen her for over three weeks."

I ran to the phone and called Shannon. She excitedly agreed to start meeting with us again. Her progression picked up over the next couple of weeks. One night after an intense discussion, she announced she had reached a point in her life where she had to choose God or death. She told us that when Rubin dropped her, it felt as if God had given up on her, and she had considered taking her own life. Now, since we started meeting with her again, she felt that God did love her after all.

She told us she wanted to make a commitment to God by being baptized. Hearing this news, Johnny jumped down from his chair, stood on his head, and kicked his feet in the air.

The evening following her baptism, Shannon planned a party at her house. Before we went, however, I first needed to give a baptismal interview to a young woman one of our county leaders had been teaching. County leaders usually did the interviewing, but they had to have someone else interview the people they taught. Besides training Johnny, I also had this responsibility.

At the church house, a timid young girl walked into the room. I said hello, introduced myself, and commenced with the interview. She was worthy and knowledgeable of the importance, significance and responsibility of baptism. But, she said that she didn't feel ready.

"I just want to prepare for a little while longer," she said. "But Ted is really pushing me do it. In fact, he is filling up the baptismal font right now!"

"Filling up the font has nothing to do with whether or not you should be baptized," I said. "If you don't feel ready, then no one should force you into the water." We talked a little while longer and determined that it wasn't right for her to be baptized right then. This news hit Ted like a slushy snowball to a blind eye. The way he glared at me, I could tell he blamed me for "throwing it."

That night, after the interview, as I sat in Shannon's trailer home, everyone else spoke happily to each other and enjoyed Shannon's dishes of banana pudding. She had made the dessert especially for me because once I told her I loved banana pudding. When she served it, however, I pecked at it a time or two and then just sat on the couch staring at the door.

My thoughts were far from the party. All I could think of was Ted's reaction to the news of my interview. "Why is he mad at me? He should be the one feeling guilty for trying to press someone into getting baptized and only caring about looking good on his report to the president. If he knew what the true meaning of baptism was he wouldn't do that. But, he is the county leader who has been called of God to lead me. So, how do I help my leader find truth? He must need love. I guess it falls on me to be the one to help him find truth by giving him love. But I don't feel love for him, so I'm the one with the problem..."

"Andy, don't you like the pudding?" asked Shannon, interrupting my thoughts.

"Yes, it's great. Thanks. I, uh, just need to use the bathroom." I stood up and walked into the bathroom. Sitting on the toilet with the seat down I put my face in my hands and muttered, "Here I go again!"

[Knock, knock] "Hey, Hogan! Are you okay? You've been in the bathroom for over 20 minutes!" called out Johnny.

"I'm fine," I yelled back. Ten minutes later I threw the door open, grabbed my bag, coat, Johnny, and another missionary who had been staying with us, Jared. Without a goodbye to Shannon or anyone else, I tromped out the door.

"I think I'd better drive," Johnny said with a shaky voice.

"Get in," I ordered, turning on the car ignition and pulling out of the driveway. I sped to our apartment, not daring to say a word. Plowing into the driveway, I burst through the door, flopped on my bed and buried my face in the pillow. Just then, our phone rang. Johnny ran over and answered. Right at that moment my mother felt impressed to call and see how I was doing. Seconds later, Johnny appeared at my side with several of my pills in his hand and a glass of water.

"Take these!" he pleaded. I took the pills and fell back on the bed. Johnny found my tape recorder, flipped in a tape and pushed play.

"Here, listen to your buddy Yoner," he said.

I listened intently until I fell asleep. About noon the next day I got up-sane again-but with severe anxiety and depression.

"I can't do it anymore," I said to President Condie on the phone.

"There's nothing wrong with going home early for medical reasons," he replied understandingly. "We'll arrange for you to return home tomorrow." I hung up the phone and slept for the rest of the day.

The next morning, Shannon took off work to come say goodbye. When she arrived, I was still in bed. Blake was there waiting to drive me to the mission home in Billings. After a few minutes, I walked into the room. Without even acknowledging Shannon, I collapsed onto the couch. From a distance Shannon watched me, trying to understand what was happening in my head. I looked over at her and asked, "Can I go home?"

Shannon walked over to the side of the couch, knelt down on the floor, took my hand and said, "What do you mean?" I told her I had done what I had come to Montana to do and asked if I could go home now.

Through teary eyes, she replied, "If that's what you want to do."

With tears streaming down my face I said, "Yes. I want to go home."

"We love you so much and will miss you terribly," she said quietly. I forced a small smile, squeezed her hand, and looked away. With that my mission ended.

Chapter 12
I'm Really Home

Dear Dawn,

Ciao! How goes your mission in Italy? You'd better hold on tight because the time is going to take off and before you know it you'll be flying back home. Speaking of flying home, I have to tell you my interesting experience of arriving home from Montana.

My parents picked me up at the airport and brought me home. As I walked through the back door Eric and Ed (my younger brothers) rushed over to give me a hug and say welcome home. They started talking a mile a minute, telling me about the latest Lego toys and funny movies that had come out. While they chattered and held their things up for me to see, I just kept on walking right past them. In a daze I carried my suitcases upstairs to my bedroom, threw them on the floor, and sat down on my bed. All I could think was, "I'm home. I'm really, really home...for good. My mission is over."

As I dwelt on these thoughts, the realization of it all hit me like a blind punch to the abdomen. All of a sudden the wind blew out of me and my body forgot how to breathe! I looked at the floor trying not to panic and expecting to pass out any second. My breaths came in broken gasps. I told my lungs to inhale, but they didn't hear. It felt like I had a short in the connection between my brain and lungs. Once every few seconds the signal made it through. In choked-up wheezes I managed to keep from passing out. Eric and Ed, who had followed me into the room and sat down on each side of me, continued talking, unaware that anything was wrong. Right then Mother came into the room, took one look at my face and asked, "What's wrong?"

"I can't breathe!" I wheezed. Realizing immediately what was happening Mother whisked the boys out of the room and sent them scampering downstairs. She took me by the hand and made me stand up. Screaming for Dad, she started walking me up and down the hallway. The walking helped a little, but I had to focus all my mind power to force my lungs in, and out, in and out. Dad came running. Mother quickly explained that I was suffering a side effect of the medication and ordered him to call the doctor.

As I stared at my feet waiting for what felt like a minute or more between each signal from my brain to my lungs that gave me fractions of a breath, I listened to Dad frantically talking to the doctor. After a few eternal minutes, he sprinted back carrying some of Mother's pills and a glass of water. Exhausted from lack of air, holding my breath long enough to get the pills down seemed impossible, but somehow I did it. A few minutes later, my memory of how to breathe slowly returned. Still in my mission clothes, I collapsed onto the bed and fell asleep.

Yeah! Some welcome home huh? Since then things are going a little better. Last week I got to go to President Watson-my Taiwan mission president's welcome home party in Salt Lake City. I debated whether I should go or not. I didn't know if he ever wanted to see me again after all I put him through. I decided to go anyway, and I'm glad I did.

When I walked into the room where he was, I spotted my old county leader from down in Chao Chou, Michael, sitting nearby. I hadn't seen him since the breakdown in Taiwan when he spent hour after grueling hour taking care of me. When I walked over and tapped him on the shoulder to say hello he looked at me, jumped up, and burst into tears! As he gave me a grizzly bear hug he asked, "Are you ok now?" After a long hug he let me go. Wiping his eyes, he said, "You came so close so many times, I really thought you were going to come out of it."

Surprised and touched at his emotional outburst, I smiled and said, "I'm okay now. A month in the hospital and a few drugs, and I'm fine."

We didn't talk much more. He just said, "I love you, and I'm so glad to see that you're well." It felt good to see him and realize he didn't hold grudges about what happened back in Taiwan.

The reunion with President Watson wasn't as emotional, but when he saw me he asked the exact same question: "Are you okay now?" I told him I was fine. We spoke briefly. I was grateful he didn't harbor bad feelings either.

Well, that's about it for now. Keep up the good work and drop me a line if you get a minute.

Love always, Andy

Yes, things were going a little better–I could breathe again. However, that was about as good as it got. Over the next few months, I struggled to establish a "normal" routine and life, but found myself fighting a cycle between depression and mania like never before.

As I woke up my body felt like an 18-wheel diesel rig trying to get started in freezing temperatures. I dragged out of bed each afternoon (that's not a typo), ate breakfast for lunch, and then cruised to work doing a night-watch job at my dad's construction site. Quitting time for the construction workers was 3:30. I was supposed to be there when they left. Many times, I arrived after 4:30 or 5:00 because I couldn't get out of bed in time. Often, I'd pull into the dusty site, look around to make sure no one was there, then lay back the seat in my car and fall asleep for another hour or two.

Many severely depressed people use illegal drugs or alcohol as an escape. I knew these were wrong and never considered them an option. However, my addiction to sleep started having the same effect on my body as abused drugs. The more I slept, the more severe the depression when I woke up. The more severe the depression, the more I longed for sleep. I came to call this the killer cycle.

Let me try to describe the feeling of extreme depression after waking up from too much sleep. Much worse than just sadness, my whole body was uncomfortable and agitated. Motivation to get up and do things and my interest in the world felt like a cumbersome load that was too heavy to carry; so I threw them overboard.

Adrenaline and energy made my hands and legs tingle and itch for exercise, but my head was too exhausted to move. My stomach screamed of starvation from meals missed while sleeping, but food looked revolting and I rarely had an appetite.

Emotionally I felt like a female at that time of the month–every day. I bawled over McDonalds' commercials, NBA basketball games (not when my team lost, but when they introduced the players), high school track meets, and listening to sappy country music. At times I forgot I had ever laughed or that I had ever felt different. Sometimes, the next five minutes were as far into the future as I could see.

Scary, obsessive thoughts constantly haunted my mind. I remember fearing death following a news report about California gangsters receiving initiation on the streets. I was in rural Utah and the threat to me was non-existent, but my mind mulled over the story so much, I really believed one wrong move could get me killed.

People often told me, "Just don't think so much." I found it impossible to do so. There are mental techniques that could have helped. However, when all this was happening, I still didn't understand or even confess the illness that plagued me. I only knew I was "down, doobie-doo down, down." Hitting the hay was the only true escape I could find.

When I had to be somewhere, I sacrificed showering and grooming so I could sleep a little longer. On Sundays, the early morning meetings started at 11:30. I usually showed up, all scruffy, with wrinkled clothes, just in time to say amen to the closing prayer. Sometimes I slept in so late I missed church completely.

Same story when school began in the fall. I signed up for late morning and even afternoon classes, but often arrived tardy or missed them altogether.

Over-sleeping also negatively affected my health by taking precedence over eating. At a road race during that difficult time, I had a fitness analyses done. The results said, of my 160 pounds of weight, I was 97.8% or 156 pounds lean and 3.5 pounds fat. My body only had 2.2% fat! The report went on to state that my fitness rating as a percentile of the population in my age and gender group, was risky. Yeah, I'd say so. Yet, I continued choosing sleep over meals.

Remember how bipolar means two poles? With all the daytime sleeping and depression, what do you suppose my nights were like? About 8:00, when most people start winding down and getting ready for bed, BING, my eyes opened wide, my mind started roaring, and any tendencies toward sleep got bulldozed over by a runaway 18-wheeler that hit a patch of black ice while speeding down a steep mountain slope. Suddenly, the sad, anxious, hopelessness changed into excited, stimulated, and motivated conquer-and-save-the-world thoughts.

During these late night hours, I wrote poetry and made long journal entries–all in Chinese. I wrote letters to Taiwan, Montana, and Italy by the dozens. I memorized hundreds of Chinese characters and studied my Chinese Bible. I thought continually about my philosophies of truth and how they applied to my life and to helping others. These manic, obsessive thoughts led to many close calls that tiptoed on the tightrope of insanity. I termed the episodes mini-breakdowns.

Mini-breakdowns happened when something–like a movie or a deep spiritual conversation put my thoughts back to the truth triangle. Although I began to recognize a breakdown when it started to happen, I still half-way believed Deity was causing it, not illness. With fear, panic and a prayer in my heart, pleading that I wasn't ready for godhood, I would dash home to get medicated before the episodes became full-blown breakdowns. I knew if I could just get to sleep, my "destroying angel" would pass by.

Nights when I was just manic and not MANIC, going to sleep was next to impossible, for two reasons. First, my mind raced from thought to thought like a sphinx moth darting from flower to flower at dusk. Second, there was the music. You hear about people with a mental illness who complain about the voices in their head? For me it was music, booming music like a record player (remember those?) with the needle and volume stuck. Even when I fell asleep, the music kept playing in my mind. I awoke feeling as mentally exhausted–as if I had danced with the boogieman all night. Night after night, my aggravated case of "I can't get this blaring song out of my head!" stole my sleep and sapped my senses.

I'm sure that while you have been reading, these thoughts have crossed your mind once or twice: "If your obsession was on God and truth, and these religious thoughts sent you into la-la land, why didn't you just give up religion? Why didn't you stop going to church, stop reading scriptures, stop having spiritual conversations, and just stay away from it all?!" I have to admit, these same thoughts crossed my mind more than once.

I wrote the last entry in my mission journal in Chinese a few months after returning from Montana. Translated, it reads:

August, 1992
Ok. I'm back. I really don't know what I can write to finish up this journal. There are a lot of experiences that happened in Montana but I haven't felt like writing them down. Now I'm going to finish this mission journal. Maybe later I'll come back and write the details of what happened in Montana, I don't know.

My life is still very difficult, but I haven't lost hope. I hope I can endure through each challenge. I hope that one day I can be on the right hand of

*God. I believe there is a God and hope that one day I can meet my Savior.
I feel that if He endured greater pain than me, then I really admire and
respect Him. Actually I know the pains He endured are far greater than
mine; I just have lost a lot of feeling. The things I know and the things I
feel don't agree right now. So there's no use writing about feelings; it's all
meaningless. My hope is that I can have the ability to endure to the end. I
don't know a lot of things and I don't know if I will continue to be like this,
but if it's God's will, I'm willing to accept it. Right now I don't feel Him, but
I still love Him.*

*I'm very happy to have had the opportunity to be a missionary for Him.
(Then in English) If I could, knowing the outcome, I'd still do it again.*

I felt caught between a rock and a hard place. The rock was my
unshakable belief and desperate need for the comfort and hope that
I only could find in the faith of my fathers–the rock of ages. The hard
place was my unconfessed illness that blamed the injections, hospitals,
pills, confusion, and depression on religious overdoses. The hard
place argued that if I left my religion I could denounce the illness. My
undeniable belief in God whispered that my faith wasn't the reason for
my depression and manic breakdowns.

I didn't know it, but ignorance of the imbalanced chemicals in
my brain was causing my whole life to be unbalanced. The result was
mentally tripping and stumbling in over-the-top spirituality. When I
was manic, I thought the "high" feeling came from doing what God
wanted me to. When depression dragged me down, I thought it was
due to sin. The conflict that I couldn't understand was, "How come
when I choose God and feel good, if I pursue the good and seek for
perfection I end up going crazy?"

Subconsciously, the choice I saw was to either "feel good, find
God, and go crazy," or "feel down, be imperfect, and stay sane."

With this ignorant mindset I started leaning more toward the
easier choice of "be imperfect and stay sane." I started doing the things
my mother had always taught me were wrong. I grew my hair long. I
drank beverages that I had never dared touch before. I watched movies
that I shouldn't have. Sometimes, I wore earrings that made it look like
I had a pierced ear.

While living with this rebellious, "it's the religion that makes me
sick so I'll open up to the world" attitude, very subtle doubts crept
into my mind like black widow spiders through an open crack in the

front door. From time to time, poisoned impressions questioned God's love for me and even His existence. I found myself thinking things like, "Following God is supposed to lift and build me. The whole missionary deal was to find joy by living and teaching others God's plan of happiness. Why, when I gave my whole heart and energy to living that life and teaching others that plan, did my bliss turn to insanity followed by a mutated life of overwhelming sadness and anxiety? If God's love for His children is as wonderful and true as I preached, why is my reward so miserable?"

Other gray and ordinary thoughts crawled in, like, "Living the teachings of Jesus is supposed to bring happiness and joy. If God is real, how come every time I feel that I'm doing good and living practically perfect in every way, it just turns out to be a "jolly holiday" in a Mary Poppins fantasy world where my happiness gets flushed away like a chalk-drawing in the rain?"

I felt ashamed these kinds of questions came into my mind. I never dared share them with anyone, or even to write them in my journal. I kept this all inside. The only indication they existed was my enhanced depression. My mind's crumbling wall of pride still stood high enough that I couldn't see over it to know that God, the Helper, waited on the other side, while my enemy, the illness, was attacking from within.

Thankfully, God did have communications with three in-tune people I occasionally allowed inside my mental wall. Side by side, these people sheltered and protected me while I fought my complicated and confusing war. The first two were my parents. Their quiet approach and unwavering support system provided me with all the necessities (and many luxuries) of life.

Unlike before my mission, they made no attempt to comment on or to control my "rebelliousness." Instead, they loved me unconditionally. I believe, because of this, I never fell away into serious rebellion and really big trouble. I shudder to think of the mess I could have wound up in if I had abandoned my family and faith, moved far away, filled my mind with violent and pornographic shows and media, my body with illegal drugs and alcohol, and then suffered an extreme manic episode. Thank God for my loving and understanding parents!

The third great source of stability was that well-loved assistant to the mission president in the Taiwan Taipei Mission. Yoner (Yoner) and I continued to send tapes to each other, sometimes more than two a week! I carried a tape recorder with me in almost everything I did, from work and school to snow skiing and dating. I told him everything. When I was manic, I spoke about my spiritual philosophies; when depressed, I spoke about my fears and plans to live a better life.

In his reply tapes, Yoner often thanked me for my friendship and shared an uplifting thought like, "I know God lives and that He loves us." Then, at the end of almost every tape, he always concluded with, "Bu yao wang ji, wo ai ni. (Don't forget, I love you.)"

I desperately needed to hear words of love and support. A year after Dawn left for Italy, her letters started dwindling. At first they came every other week. Then, after a while, I was lucky to get one in a month. The letters I received were short and generic. Mostly, they spoke of outings to famous Italian sights. Her letters seemed as cold as busted statues in a rainstorm. "She's just really into the missionary work," I thought. I continued writing weekly letters and sending care-packages and voice tapes.

Back home, I also received cold messages from Dawn's family. One day while talking to one of my high school buddies, he asked if I were going to dinner at the Fisher's house that Friday. "No," I replied, "I wasn't invited to any dinner."

"Oh really?" he asked with a little surprise. "The Fishers invite me and a few other of Dawn's guy friends over to eat with them all the time. I thought they invited you as well."

"Nope," I replied with disappointment, "they've never asked me over."

After that discussion, I decided I needed to go talk to Candi, Dawn's mother. "I bet she heard about what happened to me in Chao Chou and Bozeman and is afraid that I'm psycho," I thought. With shaking fingers, I dialed her number and asked if I could come over and talk to her.

At the appointed time, I nervously walked up to that familiar doorstep and rang the bell. Candi came and invited me in. We sat in the living room with a feeling of intensity stretched between us like cellophane wrap over a bowl of spoiled olives soaking in rotten juice.

"I hear you are taking an Italian language class," she said. "How come?"

"I need the foreign language credit for my general education requirement," I blatantly lied. In truth, I had taken every Chinese course the university offered and had so much foreign language credit that I skipped my sophomore year. I couldn't figure out how she knew what classes I was taking, and why she cared if I took Italian. Wasn't it rather obvious?

"So what was it you want to talk to me about anyway," she asked, breaking the awkward silence.

"I wanted to talk to you about what happened to me in Taiwan and Montana and let you know that I'm okay," I said, trying to sound convincing and strong.

"I heard what happened. I know you spent a month in the hospital in Provo. I know you came home from Montana early...." She paused for a moment, then looked me in the eyes and asked, "Do you still love Dawn?"

"Yes. Now more than ever," I returned, not knowing what she would say next.

She looked at something on the ceiling, sighed, and said, "I just don't want Dawn to have to support and raise a family while taking care of you at your bedside." I don't remember the rest of the conversation, but a few days later I made the following entry in my new, post-mission journal:

March 30, 1993
Last week I had a talk with Dawn's mom Candi. I tried to let her know I felt left out in their family and there was no need for that. Candi is afraid I won't be able to handle the stress of school, marriage, work, etc. and she is afraid what would happen if I got over stressed—what would happen to Dawn. I tried to show her that what happened on my mission wasn't health, but rather it was the way God got me to Helena to find Shannon. I want so bad for her to know that if I didn't feel capable of being a good husband and eternal mate to Dawn, and if it wasn't in God's best interest to see us together, I would let her go.

When it comes right down to it, it really doesn't matter what Dawn's mom thinks. So, I'm really not too concerned with it. The decision is up to Dawn. I know that if she asks the Lord for help that she will receive the knowledge of whom she should marry and (then in Chinese) I believe that person is me. Of course this is my greatest hope right now, but if the Lord tells her to marry someone else, I still support the Lord's will. (back to English) Right now though, she's on her mission and has promised to leave all personal affairs at home. So even though I miss her like crazy, I support her and try to help her while she's out. This means writing letters and sending her things that won't distract her from the important work she's doing.

With just three months left before Dawn's scheduled return, I had to find something to do to pass the time and keep me from going crazy (literally), thinking about her. I bought the sheet music of "Jessica's Theme" from the movie The Man From Snowy River and began learning to play it. It had been "our song" while we dated in high school. With my heart set on memorizing it perfectly, every night I put my mind to work plunking out each note.

The night of Dawn's return I parked my car across the street from her house. There I waited until her parents' van pulled into the driveway with its precious passenger. Through the darkness I watched her get out of the van and walk into the house. "Should I go say hello or should I wait a day or two?" I wondered. I sat in my car staring at the windows hoping to catch a glimpse of her. After a few minutes I couldn't stand it any longer. I had to see her.

Walking to the front door, I timidly pushed the doorbell button. Dawn's mom answered the door. Giving me the same look I had seen on the faces of annoyed people so many times as a missionary, she turned and called for Dawn. As Dawn approached the door, my heart started throbbing. She walked slowly looking at the floor. When she got to the bottom of the steps and came into the light of the doorway, her face seemed heavy and extremely tired. It was a kind of tired that went beyond jetlag; it was a look of mental exhaustion.

"Hi," I said quietly as I held out my hand. As if I were a stranger, she shook my hand, forced a smile then looked down at the floor. Her mom came to the top of the stairs and stood there watching. "I just wanted to welcome you home," I said. "I'll call you in a few days."

"Okay," was all she could answer.

I waited a few painful days and then called her on the phone. She spoke with a little more energy and enthusiasm, but it was nothing like before our missions. The conversations were short with many awkward pauses. There seemed to be nothing to talk about. As the days turned into weeks, we went out on a couple of dates. The first time wasn't really a date. I just told her I had a surprise and I had to come to her house to give it to her.

When I arrived, she ushered me into the living room. "What's the big surprise?" she asked. I walked over to the piano and started playing "Jessica's Theme." I had played it perfectly from memory dozens of times at home, but now as I performed, my hands got jittery and shaky. Instead of a romantic recall back to our dating days, my performance sounded like a drunk at a bar piano.

"I have the music in the bench," Dawn offered. However, I was determined to finish it by memory. By the time I got through it, any romance had long since staggered out the door.

The next date started out a lot better. It was a double date going night skiing at a local resort. We laughed and squealed in delight while carving our signature "Ss" in the powdery snow. After taking the other couple home, I drove to Dawn's house. "Would you like to come in?" she asked.

"Sure," I said gratefully. It was pretty late and the house was dark as we walked in. Stepping quietly so not to wake up the family, I followed her into the kitchen. She fixed us drinks of warm apple cider and we carried them into the living room. There we sat on the couch talking about the good old days before our missions.

"Back then, my biggest worry was a zit on my face for prom pictures," Dawn laughed.

"What worries do you have now?" I asked sincerely.

Suddenly the mood fell. "I can't say," she replied looking away.

I reached over to take her hand, but she pulled it away. "What's wrong?" I asked.

"I don't know. I'm so confused," was all she could answer.

I thought a moment. Then said, "Just for tonight, can't you forget whatever is bothering you and pretend that we're back in time before our missions?" The look in her face told me that she wanted nothing more. Sliding over, she fell in my arms, and suddenly we were back in our teenage years on our own mountain slope: Wampus. Without words, we hugged and kissed for several minutes.

Suddenly, the old grandfather clock that stood next to the couch like a giant chaperone started chiming. We listened closely as it trolled out 12 chimes. It was midnight—my high school curfew. Right then, just like the spell on Cinderella, the magic left and the smashed-pumpkin feeling of distance reappeared. Quietly, I took my cup of cider into the kitchen, dumped it in the sink, and then walked to the door. Without touching, we said goodnight. I could be wrong, but as I turned to walk away, I thought I saw a tear roll down her cheek.

That night, I couldn't sleep. All I could think was, "Does she love me or not?" The next day I drove to school in a daze. After class, I told one of my friends about the night's happenings. "I don't know what to do," I said. "I want to give her distance and let her work out whatever is bothering her, but at the same time, how can she kiss me like that and not love me?"

"You have to ask her," he said. "You've got to know."

I went to my next class but heard nothing the teacher said. Right in the middle of the lecture, I got up, marched to my car, and drove to the bank where Dawn worked. Inside the bank, I walked over to her window. "I need to see you." Surprised, she looked up.

"What's wrong?" she asked.

"I need to talk to you right now," I begged.

"Well, I'm working right now, but I get off for lunch in 10 minutes." I went back outside, pulled out a piece of paper, and started writing a letter to Yoner.

> Dear Yoner,
> I don't know what's happening right now. I just know I have to get an answer from Dawn. I'm sitting in my car at her work waiting for her lunch break. I don't know what I'm going to do. I just know that I can't go on like this.

That was all I had time to write before a very concerned and frightened young bank teller came walking out to the car. "What's going on?" she asked as she climbed in.

"Do you have a favorite place around here?" I asked in a trembling voice. I drove to a nearby park, got out, walked around the car, and opened her door. We walked through the soaking sleet and stinging fog to a bridge just below an abandoned duck pond.

"Andy, tell me what this is all about," she demanded.

I took her hand, knelt down on the soggy wood, took a shaky breath, and through tear filled eyes said, "Will you marry me?"

"Oh, don't do that," she said stooping down to her knees with a look in her eyes that reminded me of her mother.

"Well?" I asked.

"I can't," came the bitter answer.

"We don't have to get engaged right now," I cried, "I just need commitment."

"Andy, we've never had commitment in our relationship."

The scene at the hospital in Taiwan when three missionaries held me down and President Watson sat on me while I thrashed my head back and forth screaming at the top of my lungs (I was screaming Dawn's name) flashed through my head. "Then I guess this is it?" I asked.

"I guess so."

We walked back to the car and I drove her back to the bank. As she opened the door I said, "I just want to apologize now in case I say anything bad about you in the future. This is going to be very hard." She looked away, stepped out of the car and shut the door.

I started driving back toward school but, after about five minutes down the road, I slammed on the brakes, flipped a U-turn and drove home.

When I burst through the door my mother jumped up from the kitchen table. "What's wrong?" She asked with a little panic in her voice.

"Dawn and I just broke up," I said, trying to control the trembling in my voice. I threw my coat in the corner, ran upstairs to my room, and belly-flopped onto my bed.

A few seconds later, Mother quietly walked in, sat down next to me on the bed, took my hand and rubbed it, while I cursed into my pillow the words, "Wo yao si. Wo yao si. Wo yao si (I want to die)."

As I lay there, all the embarrassment, the letdowns, the depression, and everything else that had happened to me boiled over. Tears saturated my pillow. Why? Why?! Why?!! At this time in my life I was supposed to be superb, strong, and successful. I had done everything I thought great people did. I was captain on championship sports teams. I tried my best live as my church and parents taught me to. While dating Dawn I never stepped over the morality line so I could serve my mission worthily.

When my mission call came, I went to the country I feared the most. I gave it everything I had. I followed the no-music rules. I woke up extra early to study. I didn't play around. I tried my hardest to be the best I could. Why, when I finally figured the language out and started loving the people, when everything started going good, did I have it all snatched away?

In Chao Chou, I lost all sanity and dignity in front of the people I esteemed the highest. My weaknesses were laid bare, spread-eagle for everyone to see. Still, I went to Montana without complaint even though I secretly despised and hated it.

In Montana, I physically couldn't follow the same schedule I had before, but I kept trying. Right when things started going well again, I lost it again-this time, freaking out at a conference in front of all the missionaries from many counties. Still, I went back again and tried, until I couldn't do it anymore.

In my eyes, coming home six months early was disgraceful. However, I still had one hope, one love that made life bearable. Now, I had lost her as well. I felt weak, exposed, humiliated, and now-hopeless. Everything precious-my health, dignity, sanity, self-esteem, and the girl I thought I would marry and be with forever had all been sacrificed for the mission that was supposed to bring me growth and happiness.

My dream of "leaving as a boy and coming home as a man" had flip-flopped, like the guy I saw on the news who flopped on his head while doing flips on a trampoline. Like the unfortunate man in the news, I too felt paralyzed for life. How could I go on? What else could I say but, wo yao si?

Chapter 13
True Love

There seemed to be nothing left to live for, but somehow I pressed onward. For a while I tried to convince myself it wasn't over with Dawn. I thought I could win her back. A week or so later, I bought a stuffed animal and flowers, called her up and asked if I could see her. I drove over to Dawn's house, and with the gifts in hand, walked up and rang the doorbell. Dawn answered the door and invited me in. I don't remember any of the conversation, other than, when I gave her the gifts, she smiled politely and said, "Andy, I'm engaged."

After that, I wanted nothing more to do with Americans. So once again, like I did in Montana, I surrounded myself with everything Chinese. At school I made friends with a lot of wonderful Taiwanese students. I hung out in their apartments, helped them with their English homework, and watched Chinese movies with them. I was the only waiguoren (foreigner) who played basketball with their group. For nearly a year I spoke more Chinese each day than English.

Deep depression clouded out the sunshine of life in the mornings, and bouts with mounting mania, subdued only by mouthfuls of medication, continued to freeze my brain late at night. The cycle happened so often that on a tape I made for Yoner, after yet another mini-breakdown, in jest I said, "I've done it so many times, I'm getting used to going crazy, fa feng meiyou shema (going crazy isn't that big of a deal)–I just take a bunch of pills followed by a long nap, have a day or two of depression, and then I'm ready to do it all again."

In his reply tape I remember Yoner telling me in a father-like tone, "Fa feng YOU shema. Ni bu yao fa feng! (Going crazy IS a big deal; you don't want to be crazy!)" Needless to say, my life at that time was as stable as a deadly mountain avalanche.

But, even tumbling, falling, out-of-control snow has to come to a stop at some point. Almost a year after breaking up (if I can call it that) with Dawn, I received a tape from Yoner. He had finished his mission and was going to school in Hawaii. He asked if he could come and visit for the Christmas holiday. I sprinted to the phone to tell him a resounding, "YES!"

Running up and hugging him at the airport terminal felt as good as lying in front of a window in the warmth of a brilliant sun ray. Oh, it was good to see him! During his visit we stayed up late each night talking about everything from girls and broken hearts to scriptures and eternal friends. The days passed quickly, and my love and adoration for him grew just as fast. Still, I didn't realize the depth and power of his friendship until one night when we watched a video together.

I don't know why we chose to watch a children's cartoon; however, we decided to watch Disney's Aladdin. It was late at night. As we watched, in the story line I started seeing what I thought were "messages of eternal significance" straight from God, directly to me. After a few minutes, my whole body started shaking uncontrollably. Sensing something was wrong Yoner asked what I was thinking. When I told him my thoughts, he turned the movie off, took me to my room, and gave me some pills (my parents had already gone to bed and I had previously told Yoner the dosage I needed in case of trouble). Then, he took me to my bed and said I needed to go to sleep. In tears I asked him, "Why does the fate of God always fall on my shoulders?"

"Shh," he replied. "Wo zai zhili. Bu yao pa, Lin You Nan zai zhili. (I'm here. Don't be afraid, Lin You Nan is here.)" He held my hand. For several minutes I closed my eyes and let the tears and thoughts flow. Suddenly, the mania of the episode lifted. It was as if someone had literally yanked it out of my brain and flung it out the window. I opened my eyes and looked over at Yoner. He was kneeling next to my bed praying.

Up until that time I know that many people had prayed for me. I don't know why right then, right there, God answered Yoner's prayer, but I know it happened. The experience helped to convince me that prayer is a real power that can help–according to God's time and will.

That miraculous night I didn't receive complete and lasting healing. However, it was the beginning or the turning point of a new life–a humbled life with the ability to admit illness, to patiently accept imperfection, and to realize it's okay to ask for help from others. Episodes still occurred now and again. However, from that point forward, I began to see (and confess) that illness caused my depression and manic thinking, not God or spiritual imperfection.

I started to understand there were no secret messages falling from heaven that only I could see when watching movies in the middle of the night–those feeling were simply mania. During the day, when depression shot me down, I came to realize it was I who was doing the falling. The sky and the world weren't crashing down around me.

I also started admitting I needed to take medication regularly and heed the counsel of others, particularly my parents and psychiatrist. With their help, I was able to confront mania and depression honestly and squarely. I finally started to see the real causes and culprits for my thoughts and emotions. As I dealt with them head on, many changes began appearing in my tastes, personality and habits.

The first thing I realized was the huge hold music had on me. Before my mission I listened to the words of songs only while searching for a line that related to Dawn and me. I thrived on other music only for the catchy beat or cool harmonies. Now, for the first time, I started thinking about the actual messages of the lyrics.

As I consciously pondered the words of the music, songs that used to sound so rad suddenly scared me. I couldn't believe how dreary and hopeless they were. I sorted through my tapes and CDs, throwing away music with dark and depressing messages. I didn't clean it all out at once. I was still quite attached to some. But, I started weeding through them, one song at a time.

Just as I starting hearing the ominous messages in the fast food hit music (that was so emotionally weighty, not to mention expensive), I also started hearing the healthy, healing, and encouraging messages in church hymns.

"Oh, how praying rests the weary!

Prayer will change the night to day.

So, when life gets dark and dreary, don't forget to pray."

With these words in my head, I started thinking to pray when depression brought on feelings of guilt, worry, lack of motivation, or just plain sadness. In prayer I found comfort and peace.

I also started recognizing and controlling my thought-induced depression with a mind exercise I called "thought backtracking." When depression struck, rather than feel guilty and shower myself with I should be's, I started thinking to myself, "This is depression. What triggered the feeling?" Then, I followed the trail of thoughts until I could identify the source of the troubling thoughts and find a way to fix it.

For example, one day while I was cleaning out the horse's foaling stalls in my parents' barn, my emotions became as nasty and mucky as the sopping straw and mounds of manure I was shoveling. Rather than say, "I should be happy to have a job," I started an inner conversation.

"Self, I didn't do anything wrong; this is simply depression. What is the real reason I'm feeling it?"

The inner conversation continued, "I feel bad because I'm thinking about coming home early from my mission, and there's nothing I can do to bring Taiwan back."

"What made me think of Taiwan? I thought about coming home from Taiwan early when I got thinking about hospitals."

"Why did I think about hospitals?"

"I thought about hospitals because my hand hurts."

"What's wrong with my hand?" I put my shovel down, took my gloves off, and discovered an infected sliver.

The inner conversation continued, "So here's the real problem-a simple sliver. Rather than feel depressed because I can't change coming home from Taiwan early, I'll put my mind to work fixing the real source of pain."

Sometimes the depression trigger was subliminal-like the time I skipped into the department store feeling chipper and bright but stumbled out feeling dimmed and blue. Rather than running home for a nap, I confronted the depression by asking myself,

"Why am I sad? What am I thinking about?"

The answer came: "Because I'm thinking about breaking up with Dawn."

"Why am I thinking about Dawn?"

"Because the words of a country song in my head are about love flying away, up in the sky, and not being able to cry hard enough for her to hear me now.

"How did these depressing words get in my mind?"

"Oh, yeah, it's the song the store was broadcasting." I hadn't even realized I was singing along to this woe is me song. Having scoped out the source of depression, I then blasted it away by filling my mind with uplifting lyrics from a happy hymn.

More and more I noticed how positive, realistic self-talk could lift my spirits above weighty depression trying to pull me down. "Of course, my body is depressed," I thought as I hurried to school, "I didn't eat breakfast. It's okay. After I eat a good meal I'll feel better."

Even though I started recognizing depression and learned how to talk myself through it, sometimes it hit so hard I couldn't do anything to come out of it except pray in my mind, listen to hymns, or just lie down until it passed. Understanding it would pass helped tremendously.

In addition to recognizing sources of depression, I also discovered triggers of mania. I realized that when I played basketball until 11:30 at night, then came home and couldn't sleep until 4:00 in the morning, it was the late night's physical activity that induced mania. The same thing was true when I watched movies right before bed.

Conscious control of my diet helped regulate the depression and mania as well. Caffeine sodas, cookies, and candy right before bed made it impossible to sleep, and they injected the unbearable itch of restless leg syndrome into my legs. A good breakfast helped get me up and out of the early morning depression.

Even with controlling my diet and scheduling my physical activities and movie watching, minor mania in the form of rushing and raging thoughts still wreaked havoc at bedtime. During those long, sleepless nights I started saying to myself, "This is mania. Rather than lie in bed and allow my thoughts to run rampant, I'm going to get up and read a book. This will focus my thoughts and help me calm down."

Slowly, I started recognizing I wouldn't solve my family and friends' problems at 3:00 in the morning by writing them a letter. I came to understand that although I felt on top of the world, it wasn't reality. The things that seemed so vital and life-threatening right then would be watered down and manageable in the morning.

The other major contribution to the improvement of my mental health was taking my medications responsibly and consistently. I started learning the names, side effects, and other information about the pills the doctor prescribed for me. I realized that when extreme mania approached, it wasn't good to try to talk, think, or reason through it. "Get medicated and get it out of your head by doing something else" was the solution I found to be most effective.

I also noticed the time of day I took the pills influenced my ability to get up in the morning. So I took my pills at a prescribed time to help avoid falling into the killer cycle of over sleeping. Getting out of bed was still brick hard, but once I was up and going, thoughts of daily deeds replaced the heavy depression.

While recognizing and admitting I needed medication, I also experienced some very strange side effects. I started saying things I had never said before. Things like, "I need help," "I'm sorry," "I was wrong," "Let's talk about it." When I spoke with another returned missionary, fresh home from Taiwan, I thought I was speaking in tongues as the words, "That's neat you read the whole Bible in Chinese while you were on your mission. I tried hard, but couldn't do it," flowed freely and sincerely from my mouth.

I even noticed the weird side effects on the basketball court. "Nice block!" I said to the guy who stuffed my shot into the bleachers. Instead of sarcasm and criticism, I started offering compliments and kindness. The positive way people reacted to my new vocabulary and demeanor introduced a healing rainbow of light I had never known before.

Although losing Dawn made my heart bleed like a seriously wounded four-point buck, and the hunters (depression and mania) could easily pursue me by the trail of blood my heart left in the cold snow of life, I knew I must continue fighting for happiness. That meant finding my own dear.

I got set up with and dated a lot of different young women. One of them was a beautiful young woman named Sariah. My friend gave me Sariah's address saying we were a good match because Sariah had also served a mission in Taiwan. I went to Sariah's house and we had a short, pleasant conversation. She said she knew Yoner from her mission. Before I left, I told Sariah I would call her and ask her out. I left with the impression that she was intelligent, cute and everything good. However, still feeling the pain of a broken heart, I didn't call her back.

In '94 Yoner came to Utah for his summer vacation. We were living in an apartment with my old high school friend, Mark. One night, the three of us decided to go watch the new flick Maverick. Arriving a little early at the movie theater, Yoner and Mark noticed three fine specimens of womanhood sitting in front of us.

Mark recognized one of them. "Hey, Sariah!" he called out. (I didn't know it, but he had once lived in her neighborhood.) When she turned around I was shocked to see it was the same Sariah I had previously met and promised to call...but never did. I sank down in my seat and stuffed my cheeks with popcorn, hoping she wouldn't recognize me.

"Hi Mark! Yoner, ni hao! (hello)" she called out, coming over for hugs from her old friends.

"Oh, great, here it comes!" I thought.

"You have to meet our roommate," Mark said excitedly. "He went on a mission to Taiwan, too!" She looked over. I looked up. I could only wave because my face was still stuffed with popcorn. She threw five fingers at me and turned her attention back to Mark and Yoner.

"Oh, we met once...briefly," she said with a bit of sarcasm. Forgetting I was sitting there, she started talking with Mark and Yoner about old times. Sariah mentioned the next day was President Horner's (Yoner and Sariah's mission president) welcome home party. "Ni yao qu ma? (Are you going?)" she asked Yoner.

"Yes, I want to go," he answered.

"I don't have a car. Can I get a ride with you?" she asked. Yoner answered that he didn't have a car, either. Turning to me, he asked if I could take them. "Hao le (Okay)," I answered, still choked up with popcorn and embarrassment that I had never called Sariah back.

The drive from Sariah's apartment to Heber City was a good 45 minutes. The time allowed for some healthy conversation. She was even sweeter than I remembered. I felt bad that I had blown my chance to get to know her better. After the party, when I dropped her off, I thought I'd never see her again.

A week or so later, my phone rang. "Hello. This is Sariah. I was wondering if you would be interested in going on a hike with me in the mountains up above the University of Utah."

"Sure!" I answered, completely surprised she would even talk to me, let alone ask me out on a date. The hike in the hills reminded me of hunting trips with my dad in the mountains above our home. As I followed Sariah up the trail my instincts sensed that I should keep this trophy prize in my sites. Still, I knew I had to tell her about "the real me" if our relationship had any chance of progressing.

Suddenly, a distant lightning strike shorted out our hike. "That was close," Sariah said, "we had better turn around and start back."

As we hiked down the mountain, I still kept my eyes open for any opportunity for a serious talk. When we reached a point where we could sprint to the car if it started raining, I found a bony pine tree to be the perfect introduction to the skeleton in my closet.

"This pine tree reminds me of my mission," I said cautiously.

"There are pine trees in southern Taiwan?" she asked.

"No, not in Taiwan..." I hesitated, looked through the dwindling twilight at her probing eyes for a moment, and then continued, "...in Montana."

With a very confused tone in her voice she asked, "I thought you served your mission in Taichung."

"Well, I started in Taichung, but finished in Montana. While I was in a city called Chao Chou I suffered a mental breakdown and had to come home," I said quietly, fearing my words would spook her away like the snap of a twig behind a grazing antelope.

"That was you?" she asked with a surprised and intense look in her eyes.

"Yeah. You heard about it, huh...I guess word gets around on that little island, doesn't it?"

Silence.

"I just wanted you to know about my illness before we, um, take this relationship any further," I said.

"What is the illness?" she asked with concern and care in her voice.

"Bipolar disorder. It's a mental illness for which I might have to take medication the rest of my life. It makes me either extra sad or hypersensitive..." I climbed a giant boulder that rested next to the tree and motioned for her to come see the view. As we sat on the rock we talked in detail about my experiences in Taiwan and Montana.

"I've learned and changed a lot from all that," I concluded. "But I feel it's important for you to know this if we continue dating. Before she could reply, light drops of rain started pitter-pattering around us. "We'd better get to the car," I said, sliding down the rock and offering her a hand down. We sprinted down the trail. Just as we jumped into the car, the rain started pouring down.

If it weren't for the sound of the swishing wipers and splashing tires, the drive home would have been practically silent. "You don't need to walk in the rain to show me to the door," she said as I pulled up to the curb in front of her apartment.

"I don't mind," I replied.

"No, it's okay. Really. Thanks for going with me," she said opening her door and climbing out.

As I watched her hold her backpack over her head and run for the safety of her apartment, a voice in my head taunted, "You spooked that prize catch away for good!"

By this time though, my interest level in a future with Sariah had risen above the embarrassment level of my past. I determined I would not give up.

The next week, I called her and asked if she wanted to go bowling with Yoner, Mark, and me. Surprisingly, she happily, and without hesitation, agreed to go. After a fun time laughing at gutter balls and cheering for strikes, I dropped Mark and Yoner off at our apartment and then took Sariah home to hers. As we drove, the conversation turned serious. "After you told me about your illness, I went home and did a lot of thinking and praying," she said. "I feel that we should keep seeing each other and see what happens."

Dating Sariah wasn't a dazzling, dramatic relationship. Rather, we quietly enjoyed each other's company more and more. The progression felt unforced, not pressured, natural, fun, light...just right. Her love was real, and she wasn't afraid of me because of my illness. She had a way of turning the frowns of my upside-down emotions right side up again. The more we dated, the more I trusted her with my tattered heart.

Sariah's family also loved and accepted me. One night after I mentioned something about Montana, and the awkward, "didn't you serve your mission in Taiwan" question revealed my illness, her parents later told Sariah, "Well, we'll just love him anyway." After that night, they never questioned me about it again.

And so, to conclude (or begin) my love story, I take you to my favorite place on the planet: Lake Powell in southern Utah. My dad's construction company was starting a project near the Bullfrog Marina. He asked if I would be willing to pull a trailer down there for the workers to live in. I heartily agreed, called Sariah, and invited her to go down with me.

For chaperones, we decided it would be best to bring along her two sisters. I made arrangements for all three of them to stay in the marina hotel while I slept in the trailer. It was winter and quite chilly outside. That night Sariah and I went for a steamy walk where the moon's reflection in the crystal lake made her eyes sparkle like the stars overhead.

"Are your hands cold?" I asked. "You can warm them up in my coat pocket."

She put her hand in my pocket but found it already occupied. "You've got junk in your pocket," she observed.

"Take it out and look at it," I replied. She pulled a small box out of my pocket and opened it up to discover a ring. Kneeling down, I proposed, "Will you marry me?"

"Yes," she lovingly answered. I stood up and gave her a big hug. Right then I heard some squeals and giggles coming from behind a nearby rock.

"Did you hear that?" I asked with a shaky voice.

"Yes," she laughed. "My sisters are spying on us."

"No matter where I go, I'm always getting secret messages from hidden sources...and there is always laughter when I find truth," I said in a relieved, joking voice. "But this time, I'm not going to lose it." With that, I pulled my bride-to-be in closer and we kissed as if an altar was between us.

Chapter 14
Living With Bipolar Disorder

So there it is: my crazy story. If it were a movie, the romantic scene of Sariah and me kissing on the cliffs of Lake Powell would be zooming out as the love song comes to an end. But life didn't end there.

The battle with the illness that attacked me years ago in the remote city of Chao Chou, Taiwan still rages on here at home in my everyday life. I feel as if I am only barely beginning to understand this illness that has plagued me for so long. There will always be more to learn and more to tell. Here are some culminating thoughts from this point in my life.

God: I love it when I play basketball and the players pass the ball to everyone-even the guy who can't catch, dribble, or shoot very well. I love it when I see neighbors fast two meals and then donate the money they save by not eating to other families in the neighborhood who struggle financially. I love to see the youth get together and shovel snow for older folks and disabled people–without thought of compensation. I love to see my children gather with other kids at church to sing, "Tell Me the Stories of Jesus."

This kind of practical goodness comes from living God's gospel of love. It is proof enough to convince me of the value of walking in faith. But there is so much more. Believing I have a Father in Heaven, Whom

I can call upon whenever I need help, gives me strength and hope when no one and nothing else can.

While fighting my illness there have been times when I was so depressed, so discouraged, and so down, the last thing I felt like doing was praying. Sometimes all I could get out was, "Dear God, please help me." The burdens were never banished in the blink of an eye. But looking back, I can clearly see how I was always blessed with the ability to pull through.

I have learned that when I humbly and patiently ask for God's aid, help and relief always come. Not always immediately, and not always in the way I want or think it should be given at the time, but when the trial is past and I can look back and see the bigger picture, I can see it's always for the best.

Choosing to live a religious life doesn't make me feel like butterflies and flowers all the time. In fact, on the rare occasion I do feel joy, it, along with my other good dreams, always flutters away and I wake up the next morning with the same depression I always have.

Still, I know God lives. I know He loves me. I know that happiness comes from following Him. It always comes back to this. I can't prove it with a truth triangle. I can't even talk, write or think about it extensively without the spooky feeling of a manic attack creeping up behind me. However, the belief of God and determination to follow Him is rooted deep in my heart.

I firmly believe if I continue to seek God's healing ways, eventually, after the freezing bipolar winter passes, my heart's roots of faith will sprout blooms of glorious, unrestrained happiness as beautifully and naturally as the royal, purple crocus, the golden daffodils, and the ruby tulips in my mother's garden.

Yoner: I can't talk about "beautiful happiness" without mentioning my buddy Lin You Nan. His friendship is another witness of God's love and divine arrangement in my life. To this day Yoner and I keep in very close contact. Over the years the number of voice tapes we have sent to each other has reached triple digits. In the tapes we share everything: hopes, dreams, fears, trials, and weekly weather reports. Although the physical distance between us is great, our relationship continues on as strong as if we were next-door neighbors. I wish everyone had a friendship as genuine and close as ours. If they did, the world would be a much happier and peaceful place.

Parents: During growing up years, my parents often told me they loved me. I never realized the extent of that love however, until my dad spent the night with me on the hard tile floor of the drafty holding cell at the hospital in Bozeman Montana and, when Mother, seeing the unspeakable fear I had about being checked into the Institute of Behavioral Medicine, said "He doesn't need this. Let's go home."

Going through these experiences helped me to finally understand that my parents' love was true and deep. Looking back on my life, I see how they have always been there; selflessly giving everything they have for my happiness and comfort.

For so long I shunned my parents and dumped them down low on my list of priorities. Now, they are permanently perched at the very top. I believe that most youth and even adults who suffer from mental illness would do well to listen to and trust their parents. In most cases, parents are the ones with lasting love and continual commitment.

Music: Because of my illness, the medication I take, and perhaps with my just getting older, music does not have the power to move me as it once did. Sometimes I still get songs in my head that blare for hours even after I switch the radio off. It doesn't necessarily have to be music that is soft, juicy and delicious to my ears. Sometimes I just hear a song for a second or two, and it sticks in my mind like a chewed-up wad of bubblegum sticks to a curly hairdo. The only way I can dig the song out of my mind is with my prescribed sleeping pills or different-soothing (like oily peanut butter)–music.

My Bipolar Disorder: Speaking of sleeping, most of the time I still sleep in until ridiculous hours in the morning (or afternoon). I live in a country where "the early bird catches the worm." I work in an industry where "slackers" are those who can't get their lazy bums out of bed in the morning. People who don't understand the illness treat me as if my pathetic sleeping habits are a result of undisciplined habits, a weak will, or simply that I chose for my life to be this way. All this makes it very discouraging to still feel powerless as the years roll by and I very seldom embraced the warm rays of a morning sunrise.

Another unconquered symptom of my illness is scary thoughts. These mental distractions still invade my mind as often as the constant slew of email SPAM that sloshes into my inbox each day. Sometimes, before I can hit "delete," the horrendous images zap my feelings of self-worth, worthiness for heaven, confidence, and concentration into "psycho" space.

Scary thoughts hit hardest in situations where spirituality is high. It seems so contradictory! Why must my mind be filled with perversion or violence when everyone around me is moved to tears? I know the answer. My mind still harbors a subconscious fear of breaking down when I feel God is near.

I know that the intrusive thoughts don't damn me to hell, however, because the Judge of all is forgiving, understanding and loving. He knows my illness and my heart. I gained this comfort in large part from the wise counsel of a close friend. Once, I shared with this friend the frustrations I experienced resulting from scary thoughts. He told me he doesn't believe God will hold me accountable for the intrusive thoughts as long as I don't act on them, and as long as I continue to fight them. He encouraged me to view myself as God and loved-ones view me. He said, "This is the real Andy Hogan. Love him as we love you." His comforting words helped me understand and believe that my illness is not who I am. The soul inside my sick body is good, clean, and worthy. I am not "bipolar." I have bipolar.

Other symptoms of my disorder that remain with me are constant worry and mild depression. "What if" and "I should be" thinking still plagues my mind even though I know what is happening. Progress is slow. But I strive daily to combat the depressing thoughts with healthy, positive, and empowering self-talk, including many silent prayers.

Because it feels so good, recognizing and confronting mania is more difficult than dealing with depression. While manic, I'm awake, alert, motivated, and inspired. I wrote most of this book after midnight hours. It's difficult, but I am learning to catch myself before it becomes extreme. I stop, step back and say, "Whoa. I'm probably not going to win poet-of-the-year, inspire the world to change, or make a million dollars with my writing tonight. This is not reality. This is mania. It's time to slow down and sleep."

On the other hand, when I watch an uplifting movie, have an enlightening spiritual discussion, or even laugh as I run through the sprinklers with my children, I try to remind myself, "It's okay to feel good. I'm not going to go crazy. I can accept these joyful emotions. If I get too high, I always have medication to bring me down. I am in control, and I'm not going to lose it."

I long for passion, for the ability to just throw my head back and laugh, to spread my arms in the air and dance like a child in a field of seeding dandelions. I can only dream about how wonderful it would be to wake up in the morning with a refreshed, motivated, and excited mind.

Like heavy sandbags holding a hot air balloon on the ground, depression constantly weighs me down and keeps me from soaring in the clouds of bliss and happiness. At this point in my life, genuine joy almost always comes via proxy. Just as a person describes a beautiful sunset to the blind, I feel excitement and a thrill for life through those who love life.

Medication: I currently take two antidepressants in the morning, an antipsychotic before bed, and an anti-anxiety/hypnotic pill occasionally when I've tried everything else and still can't sleep. The drugs I take keep me stable and sane, but they also make my mind numb, forgetful, and less feeling. In other words they sort of "zombieize" me. When others reach for tissues at funerals, my eyes stay dry. When others scream and jump up and down at football games, I yawn. It's true the medication smoothes out the extremes of my rollercoaster of emotion. Without my meds, the roller coaster would eventually fly off the track or sink into the mud. But on the other hand, think of how boring a rollercoaster would be without any ups or downs.

Another side affect of my medication is that it causes my clothes to shrink. Even with consistent, vigorous exercise the waistline on my pants always feels tighter than it did when I didn't take my pills. Recently I heard a law firm commercial say that my antipsychotic drug can cause diabetes. Now I have to get my blood checked annually.

A lot of people think that if mentally ill people just take their medicine, everything will be fine and normal. This is a misunderstanding. On top of forcing us to live with negative side effects, the medicine allows us only to get by. It doesn't cure the illness.

Finding medication that works is different for each individual. Experimenting is risky and there are no sure answers until one tries it. I am always torn when my psychiatrist informs me that a new "improved" medication is on the market. One time I decided to try a new antipsychotic medication and see if I could improve my poor sleeping habits and lose some weight.

At first it seemed the medication was a miracle. I lost 30 pounds in one month. I felt happy and motivated–even in the morning. I started waking up earlier and earlier. Sadly, the good went to extreme and a mini-breakdown occurred. Come to find out, the new medication offered no protection. I was actually experiencing prolonged mania that grew in intensity as my old medication wore off. I suffered a whole month of extreme depression before the old medication starting working again.

When a person is fortunate enough to find medication that works, the medication most likely will be very expensive. Out of curiosity, I once figured the price of my antipsychotic medication to be $8.00 a pill! Add to that two antidepressants and anti-anxiety pills. These are expenses I will probably lug around with me for life. Medication for mental illness is far from perfect. But it is a wonderful blessing that will continue to improve as understanding of mental illness grows.

Stigma and Prejudice: If the day ever comes when my daughter dates a young man who reluctantly reports a history similar to mine, I will try not to judge and reject him only because "he's ill." Rather, I will look at how he handles his illness and then form an opinion. I will ask: Is he in denial? Does he bitterly blame everyone and everything else, or does he humbly and gratefully accept help and kindness offered to him? Does he use self-destructive habits as an escape? Does he confess his need for medication and take it responsibly? Does he listen to his doctor, parents, teachers and other caring leaders and friends? Using this test, I would hope to avoid chewing him up and spitting him out simply because ignorant fear and petty prejudice put a bitter taste in my mouth.

When I decided to share my story, one of my sour, ignorant fears was to be known forever more as "the crazy guy." Now that my history is written I have shared it with a lot of different people. So far the vast majority of responses have been nothing but respect and kindness. Not only that, but it seems everyone knows someone who struggles similarly, and all want to help.

In the opening chapter I shared the classic Chinese idiom: "jia jia you ben nan nian de jing" (Every house has a story of difficulty). This saying applies well to mental illness. Everyone is involved in one way or another. The problem is few people dare to talk openly about mental illness. My desire is that by opening up and sharing my story of difficulty, healthy conversations will follow. I believe as people communicate openly, those who silently suffer will soon realize they aren't alone, and caring company is all around.

Suicide: What about suicide? People with severe depression are at high risk to take their own life. Have I thought about it? Yes. There have been times of depression when my belief in the joyous next life made death very alluring.

During the breakdown in Bozeman, when Johnny left the car to go make a phone call, I laid the seat back and used every ounce of will power in me to suppress urges to open the door and jump in front of oncoming traffic. A voice in my mind said, "You are ill. If you die now, you will not be accountable for your actions. You can die a martyr! All you have to do is open the door and jump in front a big truck...."

Even when I was "totally whacked," as Johnny so gingerly put it, and it seemed I had no control over what I said and did, somehow I found the inner strength necessary to resist the powerful and seemingly logical suicidal urges.

I've been blessed that my body has responded well to medication, and my depression level and subsequent thoughts of suicide have drastically dropped. To those who suffer severe depression day in and day out, hour by hour, minute to minute, to those who try this medication and that therapist—all in vain—I just want to say, don't give up! Depression causes loneliness like nothing else. When I look back, even during the darkest moments that felt as long as eternity, I know I was never left alone. There is always someone who cares. Help in one form or another always shows up—eventually. Hold on! The trial will pass. Life is good and worth living.

Sariah: Now that I've mentioned the good life, let me conclude with thoughts of my precious wife, Sariah. At the time we were married, I still hadn't fully accepted that I would need medication for the rest of my life. At one point I thought I was well enough to quit taking it. As the old medication wore off, the manic/depression cycle crescendoed like the sound of rap music as the low-rider approaches.

Sariah silently suffered as I went off on manic rampages where I hounded into her ears that money could grow on trees and we could jump in the air and fly around if we had enough faith. When the inevitable breakdown was on the brink and I called her at work with the news, "I'm going crazy again!" she came home, sat next to me on the bed stroking my hand, softly singing hymns. The sound of her voice soothed my soul with stronger force than the medication I desperately downed. Even before the pills could take effect, I found myself calmed and comforted.

As time passed, I learned to rely on Sariah like a ship's captain desperately clings to his compass during hurricanes at sea. She was solidly grounded in reality and warned me when I started slipping too far away into mania. Even today, I rely on her heavily to help recognize mania and to be a source of energy when depression attacks. The distance to the sun and stars cannot compare with the depth of love that it takes to trust someone even more than I trust my own mind. However, this is the height Sariah and my relationship has flown to.

Beginning with the earliest stages of our dating, our courtship was not a romantic drama. We never even found music to deem "our song." Our relationship was more profound, more meaningful, more personal, and more sacred. While engaged and planning the type of lives we wanted to live together, we promised always to be open and honest with each other, and never to argue or fight. Friends and even family find it difficult to believe that now for over ten years and counting, we have lived up to our promise by never criticizing or yelling at each other. Of course we've had difficult times. But we either talked our way through them or bit our tongues and kept silent.

Together we live each day hand in hand, step by step. One time our neighbor asked Sariah what her secret was to living with and putting up with someone who suffers from bipolar disorder. Sariah humbly answered, "It isn't hard. Andy knows my weaknesses and shortcomings. He puts up with and forgives me just the same as I put up with and forgive him."

She doesn't like to be in the spotlight, so I'll cut short what could be pages and pages, maybe a future book, of gratitude for and tribute to her, and simply conclude with this thought: The longer I live, the higher I soar in love with Sariah.

Who knows what kind of advances in medicine will become available in the future. Who knows how long I will have to continue enduring life with bipolar disorder. This much I know: humbly trusting in God, while in living in the refining fire of bipolar disorder, has opened my eyes and heart to the true love of family and friends.

God is real. Love is the proof. This is the truth I've found. For now, it is enough.

Andy Hogan loves to personally share his experiences and lessons learned. If you are interested in inviting him to speak with your group, please visit our website, or contact us using the information below.

For Additional Copies, or Other Fine Books, Contact:

Bear Canyon Press
940 N. 1250 W.
Centerville, Utah 84014

Phone: (801) 294-3153

Email: info@bearcanyonpress.com

www.bearcanyonpress.com